in their own words

The

Beach Boys

Nick Wise

OMNIBUS PRESS
LONDON · NEW YORK · SYDNEY

Edited by Chris Charlesworth.
Cover & book designed by Nick Wise.
Picture research by David Brolan.

ISBN 0.7119.3940.3
Order No. OP 47632

Exclusive Distributors:
Book Sales Limited
8/9 Frith Street,
London W1V 5TZ, UK.

Music Sales Corporation
257 Park Avenue South,
New York, NY10010, USA.

Music Sales Pty Limited,
Lisgar House, 30-32 Carrington Street,
Sydney, NSW 2000, Australia.

To the Music Trade only:
Music Sales Limited
8/9, Frith Street,
London W1V 5TZ, UK.

Photo credits: Jay Blakesberg / Retna: 70; Camera Press: 80; Mark Hanauer / Retna: 48, 51t&b, 71c,
92, 97b; Harry Goodwin / Star File: 22b; Steve Joester / Star File: 62b; Todd Kaplan / Star File: 108t;
Blake Little / Retna: 67t; London Features International: 14r, 17, 18, 19, 23, 25, 27, 30t, 39t, 46t, 49t,
50, 60, 61b, 63b, 65t, 77, 79b, 87b, 97t, 104; Michael Ochs Archives: 8, 11, 13, 14l, 15, 16; Pictorial
Press: 5, 7, 20, 21, 35, 38, 42, 45b, 46b, 49b, 55t&b, 64, 67b, 95, 100t, 101b; Barry Plummer: 40b,
44t, 47, 54b, 69t&b, 85, 90t, 103b; Chuck Pulin / Star File: 33, 59t&b, 87t; Michael Putland / Retna:
43b, 88, 96, 102b, 103t; Redferns: 4, 24, 26, 29, 101t; Rex Features: 12, 22t, 31, 34, 43t, 44b, 53, 54t,
56t&b, 57, 61c, 62t, 63t, 66, 68b, 71b, 74, 75t&b, 76t&b, 78, 79t, 81, 82, 84, 86t, 89, 90b, 91, 93,
94t&b, 100b, 102t, 106, 107, 108b, 109t&b; Ann Sma / Retna: 108c; Scott Weiner / Retna: 99;
Timothy White / Retna: 98; Vinnie Zuffante / Star File: 105.

Every effort has been made to trace the copyright holders of the photographs in this book but one or
two were unreachable. We would be grateful if the photographers concerned would contact us.

A catalogue record for this book is available from the British Library.

Special thanks to Mike Grant.

Printed in the United Kingdom by Scotprint Limited, Musselburgh, Edinburgh.

INTRODUCTION   5

EARLY DAYS

Family   9

Hawthorne & High School   13

THE BEGINNINGS OF   17
THE BEACH BOYS

THE RECORDS   21

GOOD VIBRATIONS

The Music   39

The Band   43

Transcendental Meditation   49

Wisdom, Philosophy & Witlessness   53

SURF MUSIC AND ITS IMAGE   59

ON AND OFF THE ROAD   63

Oldies Band   69

BAD VIBRATIONS

Drugs   71

Brian's problems   75

Charles Manson   85

Death of Dennis   89

Finances   93

The Slump   97

ON EACH OTHER   99

UP TO THE PRESENT   105

AND IN MY OPINION...   111

INTRODUCTION

Few groups in the history of rock have washed their dirty laundry in public as enthusiastically as The Beach Boys. If Mike wasn't criticising Brian and Dennis for their errant ways, then Dennis was telling Mike to go take a hike, and while Brian was up to his neck in sand and dope, Carl was simply wishing everyone would stop bickering and get on with it, while poor little Al just shrugged his shoulders and shut up like he was told. And along came Bruce who took his cue and waded in like the best of them.

Sometimes they weren't on speaking terms at all; at other times they communicated only through their lawyers. Group meetings broke down in chaos and violence, lawsuits flew like confetti, vast sums of money were squandered on flippant whims... and most of the time one or another of the feuding tribe would have something profound or inane to say on the matter and the press weren't far behind.

The torrents of abuse flowed more freely as the group matured, and reached flood-like proportions with the publication of Steven Gaines' biography *Heroes And Villains* and Brian Wilson's own autobiography *Wouldn't It Be Nice*. Now everyone - group members, family, ex-wives galore, producers, managers - got in on the act. How, one wondered, did they manage to make such wonderful music with all this angst in the air?

Left, six Beach Boys: top – Dennis Wilson and Al Jardine, middle – Mike Love and Bruce Johnston, bottom – Carl and Brian Wilson.

Right, clockwise from top: Mike, Dennis, Al, Bruce and Carl.

Above: Touring during the Seventies:
Mike, Dennis, Al, Brian and Carl.

It certainly obscured the fact that from his garage in Hawthorne, Brian Wilson once transformed his two brothers, a cousin and a friend into one of the most influential bands in rock 'n' roll history. The sound of The Beach Boys truly embodied the carefree spirit of sunny California: its weather, the surf, the girls, the fast cars, the good life. With harmonies dipped in honey and rhythms lifted from the Chuck Berry songbook, they enjoyed a run of glorious hit singles at a time when British pop, led by The Beatles, ruled the world. Classics such as *Surfing USA*, *I Get Around*, *Fun Fun Fun*, *California Girls* and *Help Me Rhonda* etched The Beach Boys into the public consciousness so deeply that thirty years later they still form the basis of the group's stage show.

The crucial cog in The Beach Boys' machinery was elder brother Brian Wilson, the teenage genius who wrote all the material, played bass, sang the high harmonies and arranged the songs in the studio. Brian, it is said, simply heard things that no one else could. Emotionally fragile, shy and withdrawn, tortured mentally and physically by his father, Brian ran away into his own world of music. Eventually, he retreated so far inside, he couldn't get out... and succumbed to the escapism of alcohol and drugs. The Beach Boys' cheerful image and songs changed radically. Led by singer Mike Love, they became involved with Transcendental Meditation; led by Brian they developed a more lucid, abstract but compelling sound that was influenced by the drugs he was guzzling. Songs like *Good Vibrations* and *God Only Knows* shocked not only Beach Boys fans but the rest of The Beach Boys themselves, while the albums *Pet Sounds* and the unreleased *Smile* were fascinating not just for the beauty of the songs but for their continuity and subtlety of production. Unfortunately *Pet Sounds*, Brian Wilson's masterpiece, went generally unnoticed by the public. As a result he plunged deeper into the depths of depression, addiction and seclusion.

Declining to tour, Brian spent the better part of three years alone in his room. To get him back on his feet, the rest of the band appointed a psychotherapist, Dr Eugene Landy, to treat him. Using revolutionary new techniques to combat drug addiction, Landy twice pulled Brian from the edge of the grave and has twice been fired by the band for exerting too much control over his patient. The group continued making albums during the '70s and '80s but Brian's lack of input was clearly evident.

To add to their problems, in December 1983, Dennis Wilson, the middle brother, drowned in a California marina. Like his brother, Dennis had been battling cocaine and alcohol addiction, as well as a much publicised friendship with the infamous Charles Manson.

And still the mess goes on. Mike Love has recently taken legal action against Brian for defamation and not crediting him for his contribution on several Beach Boys songs, including *California Girls*, the most profitable song in their catalogue. As ever, the group are still eager to work with Brian again and Wilson has returned to the stage a few times but seems happier working on solo albums. The rest of The Beach Boys continue to be productive and recently scored a number one hit with *Kokomo*.

In the meantime The Beach Boys tour the world, presenting a hits package complete with surfer girls in bikinis gracing the stage. Ever optimistic, Mike stated in a recent interview that...

"Once he (Brian) pays me my dues we would, I'm sure, be successful, given the opportunity to work together."

God only knows.

The Beach Boys in the Nineties: Brian, Al, Carl, Mike and Bruce.

EARLY DAYS
Family

"My father resented the fucking kids to death. The motherfucker
hated us or he would have loved the shit out of us. It's that fucking
simple. That asshole beat the shit out of us. He just had a very unique
way of expressing himself physically with his kids."
Dennis Wilson *on father Murry Wilson*

"Brian thinks it happened when he was around ten. Some kid down
the street really whacked him in the ear. However, it's a damaged ninth
nerve, so he could have been born that way... and there's nothing
they can do about it."
Audree Wilson *Brian's mother, explaining Brian's deafness in one ear*

"Oh, I spanked his bottom, you know, like any father would do to a
kid, just whap him a little bit. No, I never hit my kid on the ear. No, no.
I was too strong. If anyone caused that rumour, all I hope is that they
have itchy piles for ten years. Because I never hit my son Brian on
the ear. Never. No."
Murry Wilson *on abuse towards Brian*

"My dad was a tyrant. He used to physically beat the crap out of us.
His big number was 'Don't ever lie. And if you lie, I'll beat the shit out
of you. And if you go outside when it's raining, I'll beat the shit out of
you'. So you go outside when it's raining, and you lie to him (about it),
and you get hit twice."
Dennis Wilson

"My dad was an asshole, he treated us like shit and his punishments were
sick. But you played a tune for him and he was a marshmallow."
Brian Wilson

"You know, few families are together spiritually and emotionally
over a piece of art."
Dennis Wilson

"My father was critical of the first thing we did."
Brian Wilson *on Murry Wilson's criticism of* **Surfin'**

"Oh man, he fought for his kids, he got them a contract at Capitol."
Audree Wilson *in defence and admiration of Murry Wilson*

"If you run out of dialogue with your manager or attorney, you
walk out... but we had a father-and-son relationship here and Murry
would not let them separate. When you disagreed with Murry,
it wasn't a manager you were talking to, it was your father."
Nick Venet *Capitol Records Producer, 1963*

Left: Brian Wilson, aged 4.

"We changed to outside management because of the emotional
strain we were under. We didn't feel that we were driving for
the things we should have been since we are in a golden position
to progress, and become possibly more successful. We felt that
even though my father had his heart behind it and had good
intentions, because of the situation you get into between father
and son, you just seem to go nowhere. It's an emotional struggle,
and that's more or less a crippled situation so we eliminated it.
It was done more or less maturely. Finally, we decided he is better
as a father, not a manager."
**Brian Wilson *on the 1964 decision to fire his father as
manager of The Beach Boys***

"There was too much tension in the family. It was difficult separating
the family thing from the group thing."
Carl Wilson *on Murry's involvement with The Beach Boys, 1964*

"He did about seven jobs, without experience, just native
intelligence. Always do better, always be stronger, always be
honest. They heard that so much... The boys just weren't happy,
they really weren't. At that time they were having growing pains,
and they thought they really knew... Murry wasn't happy either...
he was miserable most of the time... it was just a natural thing...
It happened right after they came home from their first trip
to Australia where they had lots of strife and problems...
and they fired him."
**Audree Wilson *on the rift and departure of Murry from
The Beach Boys management***

"The thing that happened in 1964, on the plane
(a nervous breakdown), it had to do with the way my dad
treated me. He was always overbearing. And it just got to
the point where I couldn't handle it any more. I'd fuck up
on something and he'd say, 'Goddamn it! What the fuck
is going on!' or something like that – a hard nosed type of guy.
He was hard on my mother, he was hard on Dennis, he was
hard on Carl."
Brian Wilson *on Murry, 1985*

"You know, since my father died, it's been a lot different. I feel
a lot more ambitious. It really does something to you when your
father passes away. Takes a while to get over it, too. I got a new
perspective on Life. I'm gonna try a little harder now...
It's making a man outta me."
Brian Wilson, *1973*

"My darling uncle didn't die soon enough. But I didn't resent
Murry any more than I'd resent anyone who stole from his kids;
beat them unnecessarily, intimidated them and screwed them up
emotionally."
Mike Love *on Murry Wilson's death, 1980*

Carl Wilson, aged 7.

"The one thing that kept our family together was the music...
The only thing that our family would share emotionally was to
have our dad cry over something the kids did with music. It's hard
to fathom that... The last couple of days of his life, he's lying in
bed, dying of a heart attack going, 'Son! You've got to play more
rock 'n' roll! Listen to this melody!' He'd get so excited."
Dennis Wilson

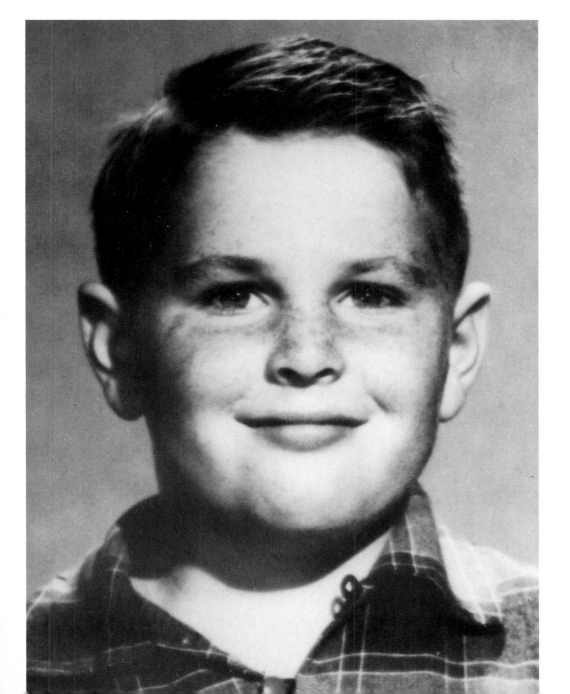

Hawthorne & High School

"I haven't learned anything in high-school anyhow. Most of my learning has come from being with The Beach Boys. The music biz is like a college education."
Carl Wilson, *1965*

"I used to have an old Rambler when I was sixteen and Mike (Love) was seventeen. We'd hang out at Foster's Freeze – that was my hangout! Everybody had hot cars; it impressed the chicks to have a pretty cool car. Mike and I, we'd go to the drive-in with a chick and before she'd know it, we'd push the button and the seat would go all the way down! It became a bed, you know? That was real funny!"
Brian Wilson

"Hawthorne, that's a crummy town, though. It was not like Bel Air or Beverly Hills. I lived at 3701 West 119th Street; it was a small house."
Brian Wilson, *1976*

"I can still remember being outside the Wilson house in Hawthorne. It was like two a.m., and here we got a tape recorder out on the lawn and peeling rubber, just dragging down the street, was this 409. Oh boy! Neighbours calling up and coming out yelling, 'Shut up!' It was a trip. We needed sounds, y'know."
Mike Love

"Brian was the oldest, I was in the middle and Carl was the baby.
I was the trouble-maker. Brian got great grades and Carl got the kind
of grades like I did. I failed everything. I was too busy fighting and
running wild."
Dennis Wilson, *1976*

"I was really a baseball fanatic. I played centerfield, and I was okay!
I really practised a lot; a lot of training. And I was about a B student
or a B-plus in school. English was probably my favourite. I liked English,
because there's a lot of tools and I guess I sensed that when I was
learning it. I said, 'Hey! this is gonna be valuable, all this English
I'm taking! Because it always pays to have a little vocabulary."
Brian Wilson, *1976*

"We were schoolmates (Brian and I). I sought him out. After we left
high school it was difficult for me because I felt very alienated from just
about everything. I felt no satisfaction for years. We parted ways. I went
to school back east and he went to school at El Camino in Los Angeles.
By the time I got out of my first year in college I had to find a musical
outlet. I had to get my thing together. I bumped into Brian on
campus one day.
    'Smash-Oh! We crossed paths. Literally. I said, 'Brian, this is it.

Above, Brian at the piano.

We have to get together'. So we went into the music room between classes and sang 'Four Freshmen' songs. When we got kicked out of the music room we'd finish up in the nurses' quarters. Then he told me more about his brothers... 'Carl, he's about twelve and really sings good and he plays guitar too'. So I met the Wilson boys and Mike Love."
Al Jardine, *1977*

"Mike had a lot of hassles with his folks. I'd be on the phone saying, 'Hey Mike! I'm gonna come to your school tomorrow at locker room time', because we used to run track. And I'd hear his dad say, 'Get off that goddamn phone! I'll bust your fuckin' nose all over your fuckin' face!' He used to say that to Mike."
Brian Wilson, *1976*

"Boy, Hawthorne was something; it was very competitive in sports. The guys playing sports there were very rough about it. But that teaches you about having to get back on your feet again and keep playing!"
Brian Wilson

"I took a music appreciation course, but the teachers were against anything except operas, symphonies, cantatas, chamber and classical stuff. Well, I wasn't going to sit there and let any guy tell me that pop music is bad. I love both. After a year and a half, I became a college drop-out and I'm not sorry. My hunger for knowledge is very strong, but I can learn more through self-study."
Brian Wilson, *1976*

Above: Al, Carl, Dennis, Brian and Mike in characteristic candy stripe shirts.

THE BEGINNINGS OF THE BEACH BOYS

"I was in the oil business for a while – gas and oil, check the tyres."
Mike Love *on his job before The Beach Boys*

"We sang in a loose structure, we sang around a piano; we didn't have any plans to become big rock 'n' roll singers."
Mike Love

"What happened in those days was something I've never experienced since. There was a spirit going down between us. It was actually magical. There was a freshness, a naïvety."
Brian Wilson *on the beginnings of the band*

"It was really incredible... It started, we went into a room and sang and it got into the air. It was wonderful."
Carl Wilson

"I made a dollar a day sweeping a laundry out. Then we made a record that was number two in Los Angeles. We got so excited hearing it on the radio that Carl threw up. I ran down the street screaming: 'Listen! we're on the radio'. It was real funky. That started it. The minute you are on the radio."
Dennis Wilson

"I guess our only ambition in those days was to form a group.
None of us knew exactly what we were doing back then. The whole
beginning was a little flimsy – we all just wanted to play music.
Brian had written a lot of songs, and I had been fooling around with
the guitar for a long time, so eventually we got together and began
doing a few dates."
Carl Wilson, *1969*

"I gave the boys enough money for food while I went away on a
three-week business trip. When I came back, they'd spent the cash on
electronic equipment. They were going to become a group.
What could I say? I became their manager."
Murry Wilson

"The Beach Boys is just a name... when we originally decided
to call ourselves that, we were thinking of water... the ocean.
For water is such a beautiful thing. I think it may have been quite
different for us all along the line if we had not been called
The Beach Boys."
Carl Wilson, *1970*

"The Pendletones! That was it, that was the first time we ever said,
'Hey, who's gonna play bass? Hey, I think I'll learn the drums!'
You know, really enthusiastic. So we'd do a song with bass and drums
and one little guitar and think, 'Wow! we're really doing great!'
And then we became The Beach Boys. A guy named Russ Regan gave us
that name. It was his idea. The name used to bother me because
I was afraid we were gonna be stuck by it, stuck with a certain label,
but it doesn't bother me any more."
Brian Wilson, *1976*

"We played at halls for men who were over sixty. It went down all right.
When you're playing you think it's fantastic. I don't know whether
the people liked it because they'd never seen anything like it before.
They all walked out, all twelve of them. But we kept on playing
and we got ten dollars between us."
Dennis Wilson

"We were just five dummies starting out. We were totally innocent
and lucked out."
Carl Wilson, *1976*

"See, The Beach Boys, the Wilson Boys, have always heard music
in their home from my writing songs and friends of ours who came
over. We were all so poor we'd just sit around singing and on
occasion drink a glass of brew. Not the children, the adults.
And then I bought a Hammond electric organ, on time, and we'd
play duets, my wife and I. And then Brian would get in the act
and sing. All they ever heard was music in the house. And on occasion
family arguments."
Murry Wilson

"It must have started on a Friday night. We used to pick up
my dad where he worked, and he'd take us out to dinner and
we used to write tunes – the family was always involved
singing together. The three of us would sing three-part
harmony every Friday night in the back seat. I think that's
where the group started. As for The Beach Boys singing
professionally, that came one day when we got the idea to
sing about surfing. My dad said he knew a guy with a garage
and we could tape record it in the garage, put it out, and
that's how we got started – very hokey. There was no real
concept behind The Beach Boys, just a couple of guys singing
about what they liked."
Dennis Wilson, *1976*

"Brian taught himself. He thinks in six-part harmony, instead
of two-or three-part. He's not only a writer, he's an arranger, and
he has a concept of harmonics which is uncanny. When Brian
was eight years old, he sang in a concert, singing one of
Mike Love's songs."
Murry Wilson

"We had no preconception that we'd be big and famous...
but the first time we thought we might be into something was
that barn in Minnesota. We had just played the second set of
four, and we stopped outside to get some air. It was totally
sold out... We saw cars down the road for a mile and a half
trying to get up – so we knew something was happening."
Mike Love

"Mike used to really dig Chuck Berry and Little Richard.
He really got into them – that's what got him into surf music.
Carl and me used to go over to his house and sit in the Rambler
at night and sing; sometimes 'til real late. Honest to God,
we did that – like, all night! First we'd be singing inside the
house and Mike's dad would kick us out, so we sang in the car.
We'd do Everly Brothers songs... "Stran-ded in the jun-gle!""
Brian Wilson, *1976*

"We stayed together basically because we grew up together.
My cousins Brian, Carl and Dennis along with Al Jardine,
are the core of The Beach Boys. We've been singing together
since we sang Christmas carols. We're a basic fundamental
family unit."
Mike Love, *1978*

"Every record had something you'd listen to – every record had
some type of twist in it that gave you the feeling that says, 'Oh man!'
you'd go to the piano, you'd say, 'How'd they do that?' Start learning
about it. It's an education! Anybody with a good ear is going to
pick on those songs and go to the piano."
Brian Wilson

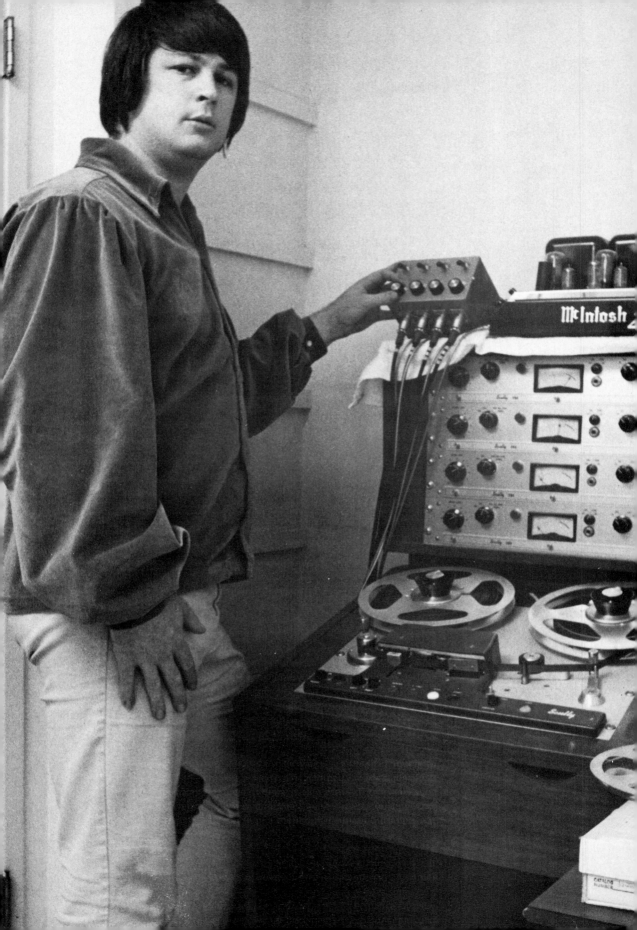

THE RECORDS

"Everything was done on a four-track basis; the first sessions
were done on a three-track. Everything was mono as far as the music
was concerned. We did all the vocals live and dubbed them.
Everybody sang at one time."
Chuck Britz *engineer, Western Recorders*

SURFIN' SAFARI

"When I hear our very first album I really laugh my head off.
I crack up because it's a comedy album. It wasn't until after the first
couple of years together that we started to appreciate what we were
really doing. Now when I listen to those early albums they bring back
good memories, as well as acting as a storage centre for information."
Carl Wilson, *1970*

Surfin'

Left: Brian with his favourite instrument, the studio.

Below: In London outside EMI house, Brian, Mike, Carl, Al and Dennis.

"We all stood around one microphone while Brian hit a snare
drum and Carl played the stand up-bass. We sang *Surfin'* and it was
done in two takes. We've been going ever since."
Mike Love, *1978*

"We were five green idiots the first time we went into a recording studio. We had a song and a dream, that's all. We sang and played our song once through, paid the guy for the use of the hall and walked out with the demo record clutched tightly in our hot fist."
Brian Wilson, *1965*

"My parents went to Europe and left us each 100 dollars for food and I bought the worst set of drums you could possibly buy. My mom had to beg the guys to let me play. I couldn't even play the drums right – Brian had to show me how on that song."
Dennis Wilson *on* **Surfin'**

"Nothing will ever top the expression on Brian's face, ever... that was the all time moment."
Dennis Wilson *on the first time they all heard* **Surfin'** *on the radio in Brian's car*

SURFIN' USA

"At Western Recorders, I remember they stood and sang for 13 hours straight to get the *Surfin' USA* album out."
Murry Wilson

BEACH BOYS CONCERT

"We were allowed one take on each number. It was a great
experience for us, playing, singing, dancing, jumping around,
making jokes and trying to look good at the same time.
Man that's a work-out!"
Brian Wilson *recalls the live recording of the album*
Beach Boys Concert, *1964*

Surfer Girl

"*Surfer Girl* is probably one of the sweetest intros to a song you're
ever going to hear. It's what you call a sweet little ballad. It had
a 'Paris Sisters' sort of sweetness. They were one of my favourites."
Brian Wilson

"There was a compulsion involved... We did it out of
compulsive drive. You see so many pressures happening
at once, and you grit your teeth... I was in a state of creative panic..."
Brian Wilson, *1963*

"*Surfer Girl* is my favourite Beach Boys' song. I liked the
melody and I liked the music. It was the first ballad we ever did;
we actually recorded it before *Surfin'*, though we didn't release
it 'til much later. We did it without knowing how; it was the first
time we ever did a song like that. It was an innocent recording
experience."
Brian Wilson, *1976*

I Get Around

"I never even heard *I Get Around* until Brian played it in the studio."
Carl Wilson, *1965*

"Just because a certain style sells in one year, it's not necessarily
going to sell in the next. We'd moved on, evolved and changed.
Witness the first verse of *I Get Around* - 'I'm getting bugged driving
up the same old strip, I've got to find a new place where the kids
are hip' – hip meaning awareness."
Mike Love

"*I Get Around* – What it meant was we had experienced
a great deal of commercial success in terms of going around
the world first class, tons of cars, nice houses, ladies, this and
that, and yet there was something more to it than that.
That's just the superficial material value of life and although it's
beautiful and we're not knocking it, that wasn't it, you know."
Mike Love

Fun Fun Fun

"We rehearsed *Fun Fun Fun* only once before we needled it
on wax."
Carl Wilson, *1965*

"We were in a cab going from the Holiday Inn in Salt Lake City
to the airport... I got the idea to do a song about a girl who borrows
the car from her father and instead of going to the library like she tells
him, goes cruisin' to see and be seen by all the boys. Her father finds
out she didn't go to the library; she went to the hamburger stand.
Yet when he takes the car keys away, the guy says, 'Well, that's
okay because now we'll have fun fun fun, now that daddy took the
T-Bird away'."
Mike Love

Little Honda
"I remember when we did *Little Honda*, Brian wanted to get this
real distorted guitar sound, real fuzzy. 'This guitar sounds like shit',
I said and he goes, 'Just do it'. When I heard it, I felt like an asshole.
It sounded really hot. That was before fuzz became a big deal."
Carl Wilson

Surfin' USA
"With *Surfin' USA*, we developed grace and style. For the first time
we used modern techniques, singing twice, the second time exactly
on top of the first, perfectly synchronized. This gives a rather shrill
and magical, much brighter, more gutsy and spectacular sound.
Professionally we were coming of age."
Brian Wilson, *1965*

Help Me Rhonda
"It was *Rhonda* I had difficulty with... It was the second I sang
lead on; I was used to singing background. It was a whole different
thing... quite complex. It seems quite simple now but it's something
called timing metre, and rhythm. It was a matter of getting your
mind-body concentration together... Finally it came together real well.
The way we cut the first version was different than the way we sang the
second. When Gary Usher decided he might want to cover it, we decided
to get a version out first. So Brian raced in and said,'Let's do it again'."
Al Jardine

Shutdown
"*Shutdown* means when you win a race, you shut them down."
Carl Wilson

California Girls
"It kind of represents California living. It's so centred on California.
It has to do with my interest in girls. There's nothing greater than
a girl... Well a kid, your daughter, but that's a girl too. It reflects my
philosophy. It's kind of a high point of Mike Love's career... It features
Mike Love as a great rock-and-roll singer... not to mention that it
has some good harmony, plus a good background track. If you listen,
you'll hear that the instruments are playing really nice. We had
a lot of musicians supporting The Beach Boys, including a lot of
Phil Spector's musicians."
Brian Wilson, *1979*

"People are part of my music. A lot of my songs are the result
of emotional experiences, sadness, pain, joy and an exultation in
nature and sunshine and so on... like *California Girls* which was a
hymn to youth."
Brian Wilson, *1966*

PET SOUNDS

"There was a natural creative progression with Brian... Recording
techniques evolved which allowed us to stretch out even more in
terms of sound textures. Brian took advantage of that and pioneered
his way through. He blended symphonic arrangements with rock
music in *Pet Sounds.*"
Mike Love

"I never objected to musical progressions... the only thing I ever
objected to was lyrics – I think lyrics should be used to communicate.
Music or sound which will communicate a feeling. Meaning and feeling
together make a musical whole... Although I thought they were far-out,
I didn't relate to them. When I heard a lyric that didn't make sense,
I could appreciate it on an aesthetic level, but it didn't sit right with me.
I had a difference of opinion from those who did."
Mike Love

"I think they thought that it was for Brian Wilson only. They knew
that Brian Wilson was gonna be a separate entity, something that was
a force of his own, and it was generally considered that The Beach Boys
were the main thing. So with *Pet Sounds* there was a resistance in that
I was doing most of the artistic work on it vocally, and for that reason
there was a little bit of intergroup struggle. It was resolved in the fact
that they figured that it was a showcase for Brian Wilson, but it was
still The Beach Boys. In other words, they gave in. They let me have
my little stint."
Brian Wilson, *1976*

"I was very proud of that album. The reason we made *Pet Sounds*
was because we specialised in certain sounds. I don't know how
many months we spent working hard on that album to get
all those different cuts just right. It was our best – the songs
were our pet sounds. It was kind of a silly thing, but *Pet Sounds*
just made me think that you could do a whole album that was
a bitch; that held together and was not simply a collection of
various songs."
Brian Wilson, *1976*

"Oh boy, he (Brian) was so proud of it. People weren't ready for it –
it was too much of a shock, but a lot of people who understood it really
loved it. He just told me one night, he said, 'Marilyn, I'm gonna make
the greatest album ever made', and he meant it. Boy he worked his
butt off when he was making *Pet Sounds*.

   "And I'll never forget the night that he got the final disc, when it
was finished. We went into the bedroom where we had a stereo, and
we lay there all night on the bed, and just listened and cried and did
a whole thing. But *Pet Sounds* was not a big hit. That really hurt him
badly, he couldn't understand it. It's like, why put your heart and soul
into something?"
Marilyn Wilson *Brian's wife, 1966*

"I felt that the production was a masterpiece. *Pet Sounds* was
an offshoot of the Phil Spector production technique. I'm proud
of it for that reason, in that we were able to produce tracks
that had a monumental sound to them. It had that wall of sound
touch to it.

   "My contribution was adding the harmonies, learning to
incorporate harmonies and certain vocal techniques to that Spector
production concept that I learned. But *Pet Sounds* wasn't really
conceived as a 'concept album'. It was really a production concept
album. It wasn't really a song concept album or lyrically a
concept album."
Brian Wilson, *1976*

"I thought Brian was screwing up. He was no longer looking
to make records, he was looking for attention from the business.
He was trying to torment his father with songs his father couldn't
relate to and melody structures his father couldn't understand."
Nick Venet's *first reaction to* **Pet Sounds,** *1966*

Wouldn't It Be Nice
"Now, there's another track called *Wouldn't It Be Nice* which
has a very special and subtle background and for a very long time,
I thought it would be the single after *Sloop*. But that was before
Good Vibrations. One of the features of this record is that Dennis
sings a special way, cupping his hands. I had thought for hours of
the best way to achieve the sound and Dennis dug the idea because
he knew it would work."
Brian Wilson

That's Not Me

"I think *That's Not Me* from *Pet Sounds* reveals a lot about
myself... just the idea that you're going to look at yourself and
say, 'Hey, that's not me'. You're going to get your identity clear,
kind of square off with yourself, say this is me, that's not me.
That explains it."
Brian Wilson

Let's Go Away For A While

"I know I'm a creative man, musically – from early days
I believed... I think that on *Pet Sounds* the track *Let's Go
Away For A While* is the most satisfying piece of music
I have ever made. I applied a certain set of dynamics through
the arrangement and the mixing and got a full musical
extension of what I'd planned during the earliest stages
of the theme.

"I think the chord changes are very special. I've used a lot
of musicians on the track – twelve violins, piano, four saxes, oboe,
vibes, a guitar with a Coke bottle on the strings for a semi-steel-
guitar effect. Also, I used two basses and percussion. The total
effect is... 'Let's go away for a while'. Nice thought. Most of us
don't go away, but it's still a nice thought.The track was supposed
to be the backing vocal but I decided to leave it alone. It stands
up well alone."
Brian Wilson

God Only Knows

"*God Only Knows* was a song that was written in twenty minutes."
Brian Wilson, *1988*

"*God Only Knows* wasn't the best record ever made. But
if you take it as a song, you got something going. You got
something going because then you can hear the melody and
the chords. It's not a great Beach Boys record. But it's still
a great song."
Brian Wilson, *1988*

"I think *God Only Knows* explains a lot about me in that I believe
in God, and I am humble enough to say God knows what I would
be without whoever I was talking about... But it just goes to show
feelings. When you believe in something you reflect it in your
songs. You say how you feel, and songs don't lie. Songs are the
most honest form of human expression there is – there's nothing
that lies about a song."
Brian Wilson

I Just Wasn't Made For These Times

"*I Just Wasn't Made For These Times* reflects my life. It was
about a guy who was crying because he thought he was too
advanced and he'd eventually have to leave people behind."
Brian Wilson

Caroline No

"See, a lot of people don't know it, but that song was about a girl that
Brian was really in love with in high school, named Caroline. He saw her
again years later and it all came back to him, and he wrote the song."
Dennis Wilson

Hang On To Your Ego

"I probably said, this is a bullshit statement, you guys are just fucked up
on drugs, and I probably didn't sing it. The thing about the ego was you
take acid and you get rid of your ego, and I wasn't interested in taking
acid or getting rid of my ego. Brian did that, to a degree, and ruined
himself in terms of his dynamic, and the competitive side of his psyche
went down the drain about 1968 or '69, when he began to over-indulge
in those sorts of things."
Mike Love, *on why he refused to sing* **Hang On To Your Ego**
until the lyrics were changed, 1993

Heroes And Villains

"That was a cool record, that really was. Except the singing sounds
a little like I was trying to take a shit. 'I been in this town so long!'
You know? Take a shit right on that record right there, Wilson.
Now it wasn't that bad when you really think about it."
Brian Wilson, *1988*

Good Vibrations

"I was very upset by the failure of *Pet Sounds* and I wanted to be certain
that *Good Vibrations* was flawless before we released it."
Brian Wilson

"The other guys couldn't understand a lot of what were doing. I was using
a Moog synthesizer, almost unknown in those days, which made noises like
something out of a science fiction movie. I remember Carl saying to me:
'We've been on this song for months and it doesn't even sound like music!
God knows what will happen if it doesn't work out. Every cent we've got is
in it.' I told him, 'Just trust me and it will work out OK,' and it did."
Brian Wilson

"I wanted to see what I was capable of doing. I tried to reach a personal
pinnacle of writing, arranging, and producing with *Good Vibrations*.
It took six months to make. We recorded the very first part of it at
Gold Star Recording Studio, then we took it to a place called Western,
then to Sunset Sound, and then to Columbia. We wanted to experiment
using four different studio sounds. Every studio had its own marked
sound. Using the four studios had a lot to do with the way the final
record sounded. So it took quite a while."
Brian Wilson, *1976*

"I remember the time we had it... I remember I had it right in the sack.
I could just feel it when I dubbed it down to mono. It was a rush –
a feeling of artistic beauty."
Brian Wilson

"There was a lot of 'Oh, you can't do this, that's too modern' or 'That's going to be too long for a record'. I said, 'No, it's not going to be too long a record, it's going to be just right'."
Brian Wilson

"I think that *Good Vibrations* was a contribution in that it was a pocket symphony, it had a pocket symphony effect... It was a series of intricate harmonies and mood changes. We used a 'cello for the first time in rock 'n' roll, so I think in that respect it was an innovation."
Brian Wilson, *1976*

"It had a lot of riff changes... movements... It was a pocket symphony – changes, changes, changes, building harmonies here, drop the voice out, this comes in, bring this echo in, put the theremin here, bring the 'cello up a little louder here. It was the biggest production of our lives!"
Brian Wilson

"We wanted to do something that was R&B but had a taste of modern, avant-garde R&B to it. *Good Vibrations* was advanced rhythm and blues."
Brian Wilson

"I can remember doing 25-30 vocal overdubs of the same part, and when I say part, I mean same section of a record, maybe no more than two or three seconds, four seconds, five seconds long..."
Mike Love, *1966*

"My mother used to tell me about vibrations, and I didn't really under-stand too much of what she meant when I was a boy. It scared me to death... So we talked about good vibrations with the song and the idea, and we decided that on the one hand you could say... those are sensual things. And then you'd say, 'I'm picking up good vibrations', which is a contrast against the sensual, the extra-sensory perception that we have. That's what we're really talking about."
Brian Wilson, *1966*

"When I heard the *Good Vibrations* track it really zonked me out. We heard it on playback at Western Recorders. We were playing it for Russ Regan, a guy in the record industry out there... It was a very heavy R&B track. The first track Brian kept was so R&B it sounded like Wilson Pickett would be recording it. It was so far out. Then we did sections of a track, and finally we were satisfied with enough sections, you know, a cappella things and harmony things with the tracks, and it culminated in what came out, the edited single version of *GV*. There's a track laying around somewhere that would be far out to hear someone like James Brown do. You know, with those freaky horn things they do and some girl singers in the back."
Mike Love

"On one passage of one little thing on *Good Vibrations*, we did it over and over and over and over... and not only was it to get the note, we wanted the notes right, but the timbre and quality of each note, and how the four parts would resonate together, and then Brian would be hearin' something that nobody could hear includin' a dog, ya know?... and he would say 'Do it again', and we'd say, 'Do it again? What, are you crazy?'... and it was exhausting, but it came out pretty good."
Mike Love, *1966*

"I think when we finally heard *Good Vibrations* edited, mixed, we thought we were gonna have the biggest hit in the world or the career was over."
Bruce Johnston, *1966*

"When *Good Vibrations* was forming itself in my mind, I could hear the theremin on the track. When it became obvious that this would be a single, I had our equipment manager order us a small, compact model so that Mike could play it on stage.

"He moves a lever up and down a scale – it sounds like a woman's voice. Or like a violin bow on a carpenter's saw. You make it waver, just like a human voice and... well it's groovy!"
Brian Wilson, *1966*

"The whole idea behind *Good Vibrations* was that we were setting out to create a record that everybody would spook to. It would scare people and that would be a really heavy record. And what we did was, we got so into it that the more we created, the more we wanted to create.

Above: Brian takes a dip and shows off his gold album for 'Endless Summer', the compilation album that hit number one in 1974.

You know what I mean? And the whole goddamn deal just came together like gang-busters. That record came together like nobody's business. That was one of our heaviest records that we ever made, if not 'the' heaviest record we ever made. And we'll ever make."
Brian Wilson, *1986*

SMILE

"He was over-acidized. I like some of his alterations and some of the, what do you call it, allusions and delusions, allusions and all that stuff was good, but on the other hand I always thought if you're going to write something it ought to make some sort of sense. To me a lot of it did, some of it did, and some of it didn't."
Mike Love *on Van Dyke Parks' lyrical contributions*

"I could appreciate the brilliance of the music. Like with *Good Vibrations,* the music was completely unique and weird to some, but I wrote the words so it would relate to a larger group of people, because the track was pretty out there for 1966, y'know? I would always try to connect with some meaning for the listener, whereas that was not the goal with Van Dyke Parks. I called it 'acid alteration' at the time."
Mike Love, *1993*

"Because we got off on bags that just fucking didn't have any value for vocals! A lot of tracks just weren't made for vocals, so the group couldn't do it! We got really stoned! We were too fucking high, you know, to complete the stuff! We were stoned! You know stoned on hash 'n' shit!... I had to! I had to! It was destroying me! I was being destroyed thinking about it! It just wasn't my type of music!"
Brian Wilson's *first explanation of why he apparently destroyed the Smile master tapes, 1976*

"Oh well, that was because... the lyrics, Van Dyke Parks had written lyrics that were, it was all Van Dyke Parks and none of The Beach Boys. The lyrics were so poetic and symbolic they were abstract, we couldn't... Oh no, wait it was, no really, I remember, this is it, this is why, it didn't come out because I'd bought a lot of hashish. It was a really large purchase, I mean perhaps two thousand dollars' worth. We didn't realise, but the music was so influenced by it, the music had a really drugged feeling...

"I mean we had to lie on the floor with the microphones next to our mouths to do the vocals. We didn't have any energy. I mean you come to a session and see the group lying on the floor of the studio doing the vocals, you know, you can't..."
Brian Wilson's *second explanation of why* **Smile** *never came out*

"We never finished it, because a lot of that shit just bothered me – but half of it we didn't finish anyway. Van Dyke Parks did a lot of it, and we used a lot of fuzz-tone. It was inspiring, because Van Dyke is a very creative person, and it was a boost to me because he had a lot of energy and a lot of fresh ideas, so that energy has helped me.

But a lot of stuff was what I call little segments of songs, and there was a period when I was getting stoned and so we never really finished anything. We were into things that just didn't have any value for vocals, tracks that weren't made for vocals, so the group couldn't do it."
Brian Wilson's *third explanation of why* Smile *never came out*

"Well we got a little arty about it, and it got to the point where we were too selfishly artistic and we weren't thinking about the public enough. It got to that level. Partially because of the drugs..."
Brian Wilson's *fourth explanation of why* Smile *never came out, 1976*

"We didn't finish it because we had a lot of problems, inner group problems. We had time commitments we couldn't keep, so we stopped. Plus for instance, we did a thing called the *Fire Track*. We cut a song called *Fire* and we used fire helmets on the musicians and we put a bucket with fire burning in it in the studio so we could smell smoke while we cut. About a day later a building down the street burned down. We thought maybe it was witchcraft or something, we didn't know what we were into. So we decided not to finish it. Plus I got into drugs and I began doing things that were over my head. It was too fancy and arty and was doing things that were not Beach Boys at all."
Brian Wilson's *fifth explanation of why* Smile *never came out*

"During the recording of the album which was to have been released under the name *Smile*, Brian Wilson composed a piece of music known as *Mrs O'Leary's Cow,* but the legend referred to it as *Fire*. The music simulated fire itself, and was performed by leading Los Angeles studio musicians under the direction of Brian and Van Dyke Parks. Brian's wife, Marilyn, recalls rushing about Los Angeles purchasing firemen's hats for the musicians on the day of the session.
    "The music is stimulating, and to some frightening. A short time after the track was recorded, there were, coincidentally, a number of fires in the LA area. Whether they contributed to the year long delay in- the release of material intended for *Smile* or not, cannot be proven. The tapes of the recording session were never destroyed."
A Warner Brothers press release explains the mysterious occurrences involved with the famous *Fire* tapes. Brian was so shaken by the outbreaks of real fire and by the song itself, he felt the public should never be subjected to the song. To this day he maintains he personally destroyed the masters

"They're all vignettes. You see, that's Brian Wilson's greatest work – not the sustained riffs of a blues band, but the little musical vignettes – ten or twenty seconds of verse, a chorus, a shot here or there and then out. And that's what the whole *Smile* era was – vocal trips, musical trips, little trips, experiments, they'd go down this alley and maybe it would be a dead end. It didn't mean it wasn't good, it just didn't fit with something, and sometimes they were dropped. Sometimes things fit together and sometimes they were dropped. There's no way it could be made sensible and logical. It doesn't follow any pattern you could trace."
Mike Love

Above: Carl.

"The album was never completed. The *Fire* tapes were 'not' destroyed and all that kinda crap."
Carl Wilson, *1976*

"Brian was consumed with humour at the time and the importance of humour. He was fascinated with the idea of getting humour into a disc and how to get that disc out to the people."
David Anderle *friend of Brian's and founder of Brother Records, talking about Brian's inspiration on the 'abandoned'* Smile *album, 1966*

"You're going to blow it Brian. Stick to the old stuff. Don't fuck with the formula."
Mike Love *after hearing the* Smile *sessions, 1966*

Riot (Student Demonstration Time)
"Maybe one day I'll make music of my own. And the last song I'll ever play drums on is *Riot*. After we recorded that, I cut my hand. All the nerves were severed and I can't play drums any more. I lost all the nerves in my thumb and first finger. Those are the two fingers I hold the drumstick with in my right hand. I have no strength or feeling there. I play 30 seconds before the stick slips out. They say it'll take three years for the nerves to heal up."
Dennis Wilson, *1971*

Wild Honey
"*Wild Honey* was simply music to cool out by. Brian was still very spaced out, though I seem to recall he'd given up acid by that time. His thing with acid was short but very intense, plus we, the whole band, were smoking this very heavy dope. That's why *Smiley Smile* sounds the way it does. But we all really dug Motown, so Brian reckoned we should get more into the white R&B bag. I also recall around that time the band, and Brian in particular, getting criticised very heavily for sounding like choir boys."
Carl Wilson

SURF'S UP

"I was writing songs a lot while I was with The Beach Boys, but most of them I never showed to the group. I felt that if I filled in an album with two or three songs each time, that would keep songs that we might be lucky enough to get from Brian out, so I just decided to stay low.
   "I felt that one of the reasons it wasn't happening for us record-wise in the late 60's and early 70's was because of the fact that Brian wasn't into it, and because of his lack of contributions. When you have a Brian Wilson in your group and he's not productive, it's gonna be tough to sell, because he created such an incredible legacy.

Below: Al.

"I know that when we took *Surf's Up* and patched it together to finally get it out, I came up with some vocal parts in the style of what Brian would have done. It got to a point where we were writing and arranging in the style of Brian Wilson, because he really wasn't actively involved. It really got ridiculous."
Bruce Johnston, *1976*

Surf's Up
"It's a man at a concert; all around him there's the audience, playing their roles, dressed up in fancy clothes... The music begins to take over. 'Columnated ruins domino'. Empires, ideas, lives, institutions – everything has to fall, tumbling like dominoes... 'Canvas the town and brush the backdrop'. He's off in his vision, on a trip. Reality is gone... A choke of grief. At his own sorrow and the emptiness of his own life, because he can't even cry for the suffering in the world, for his own suffering. And then hope. *Surf's Up!*"
Brian Wilson, *1966*

SUNFLOWER

"Well *Sunflower*, I'd say, is the truest group effort we've ever had. Each of us was deeply involved in the creation of almost all the cuts. Say, someone would come to the studio early and put down a basic track, and then someone else would arrive and think of a good line to overdub."
Carl Wilson, *1970*

"*Sunflower* is the last real Beach Boys album, simply because it's the last album Brian personally directed – the last album which recognized the need for a monarchial figure to be up there calling the shots as opposed to the pussyfooting democracy which ended up splitting all their subsequent albums into sections."
Bruce Johnston *who left The Beach Boys during the making of* **Carl And The Passions – So Tough***, shortly after the* **Sunflower** *album in 1972*

"It was a lot easier than trying to do *Smile*. It never came out 'cos it was too difficult so... there was so much... er... it was just very difficult, so... oh, *Sunflower* was really a snap, you know, as far as ease. We didn't do it quickly, it just sort of had its own flow. We recorded more things than we released on it and... er... just, you know, decided to release it when we had that particular collection of songs."
Carl Wilson, *1970*

HOLLAND

"Brian thought up the idea of the fairy tale in Holland, and we all thought it was great how the whole thing came together. We all loved working on it, and from the start we thought it made a great little 'present' to go with the album."
Mike Love *on the Brian Wilson fairy tale entitled* **Mount Vernon And Fairway** *which was included on the* **Holland** *album*

"Well, we were in another country, in Holland, and I just sat
around and drank apple sap – that's like apple cider – and just sat
around and just dreamed. And one night I was listening to that
Randy Newman album *Sail Away,* and I was sitting there with a
pencil and started writing. And I found that if I kept playing the
Randy Newman album, I could still stay in that mood. It was the
weirdest thing – I wrote the whole fairy tale while listening to
that album.
    "I was thinking about Mike Love's house, and I just wrote,
'There was a mansion on the hill', and then later on, in my head,
I created a fairy tale. But nobody was ready for it, nobody. I remember,
Carl said, 'What!?' I wanted it to be on the album, but they (the group)
said, 'No it's too long'. We argued and all, and I was depressed. So they
finally compromised by saying, 'O.K, we'll slip it in the package as an
extra record or something."
Brian Wilson *on* **Mount Vernon And Fairway**

"I can remember that around 1957 or '58, Brian had an old
Rambler, and he used to come over to my house a lot to hang out
and sing. I was living at the corner of Mt. Vernon and Fairway in
the View Park/Baldwin Hills section of Los Angeles at the time.
You know that line in Brian's fairy tale about 'distant lights'?
Well that was from my bedroom upstairs, which had a fantastic view.
We used to sleep in the bunks, and I'd have a transistor radio on
under the covers so we could listen to the late night R&B on KGFJ
and KDAY. You remember that part in the fairy tale about the 'prince's
magic transistor radio'?"
Mike Love *on* **Mount Vernon And Fairway**

BEACH BOYS IN CONCERT

"The live album is good. We wanted to get something on there from
all the different eras of The Beach Boys, and I think it worked out well
in being a very representative album. You get almost the total feeling
of a concert, except the crowd noise gets mixed down a little bit.
Obviously on a live record there are points where we could have
done a solo better, but that's only to be expected."
Mike Love, *1974*

SPIRIT OF AMERICA

"I approved of the fact that it sold a million."
Mike Love *on being asked what he thought of Capitol releasing
the* **Spirit Of America** *album without their approval, 1975*

15 BIG ONES

"I personally ran out of ideas and turned to some old stuff,
and thought, hey, for the time being, it's cool just to do old ones.
There's not a lot of new stuff."
Brian Wilson, *1976*

"There is going to be basic disapproval (when the album comes out). People will say the group copped out of the writing derby."
Brian Wilson, *1976*

"I looked at the guys and they looked kinda sad. They didn't look happy, they looked like something was wrong. I said to myself, 'Hey maybe they're upset because we're not having any hit singles! Maybe they're mad at me!'"
Brian Wilson, *1976*

"The truth is, Dennis and I were hoping that Brian would go back to the main plan. Dennis and I had a picture of doing an album of oldies just as a warm up and then doing another album. But as it happens we started out to do the new stuff and then Brian said, 'Well, I've recorded enough. I don't want to record any longer and the album's finished'."
Carl Wilson, *1976*

"We were heartbroken. People have waited all this time, anticipating a new album – I hated to give them this. It was a great mistake to put Brian in full control. He was always the absolute producer, but little did he know that in his absence people grew up. We became as sensitive as the next guy. Why should I relinquish my rights as an artist? The whole process was a little bruising."
Carl Wilson, *describing his disappointment at* 15 Big Ones, *1976*

"Lately I have found it difficult as heck to finish a song. It's a funny thing. Probably not much of a song left in me... if any, because I've written so many, some 250 songs or 300 or whatever it is. And the creativity just doesn't seem as vast... That's why we did a lot of oldies but goodies this time on our album. That got us going, as a matter of fact."
Brian Wilson, *1976*

BEACH BOYS LOVE YOU

"Of the fourteen songs on the album, I sing six – I can't remember which ones though. I think my favourite songs on the album are *Airplane* and *The Night Was So Young*."
Brian Wilson, *1977*

"My psychiatrist took me to the studio and put me on a programme of songwriting. He just said, 'I want you to write songs. That's your job in life, you're supposed to write songs, and you might as well just sit down and start writing songs'. I said 'All right, I'll give it a try'. So I sat down and I wrote a song a day for 14 or 15 days."
Brian Wilson, *1977*

"*15 Big Ones* was harder. We had a difficult time amongst us. We squabbled a lot and there were strange weird feelings that kind of fucked me up. I got through it."
Brian Wilson, *1977*

Below: Brian on stage in the Seventies.

MIU

"We had an invitation from the Maharishi himself to record at
his facilities. We wanted to do something different so we accepted.
We renovated Building 154 of the university, put in a cafeteria, dorm
rooms, a studio in the basement, and did most of the arranging, singing,
and writing there. It also gave our wives and children a fresh dip into
TM while we worked."
Al Jardine, *1978*

"I hope that the karma will fuck up Mike Love's meditation for ever.
That album is an embarrassment to my life. It should self- destruct."
Dennis Wilson, *1979*

In January, 1975, Circus *magazine asked Carl and Mike
who sang the leads to their most popular songs. Here are
their answers:*

Surfin'... *Mike*
Surfer Girl... *Brian*
Little Deuce Coup... *Mike*
I Get Around... *Mike*
Don't Worry Baby... *Brian*
California Girls... *Mike*
Sloop John B... *Brian and Mike*
Good Vibrations... *Carl*
God Only Knows... *Carl*
Wouldn't It Be Nice... *Brian*
Be True To Your School... *Mike*
In My Room... *Brian*
Help Me Rhonda... *Al*
Surfin' USA... *Mike*
Shut Down... *Mike*
Surfin' Safari *Mike*
409... *Mike*
Fun Fun Fun... *Mike*
Heroes and Villains... *Brian*
Wild Honey... *Carl*
Caroline No... *Brian*
Darlin'... *Carl*
Do It Again... *Mike*
I Can Hear Music... *Carl*
All I Want To Do... *Mike*
Add Some Music To Your Day... *Mike*
Slip On Through... *Dennis*
Tears In The Morning... *Bruce Johnston*
Cool Cool Water... *Brian*
Deirdre... *Bruce*
Marcella... *Carl*
Sail On Sailor... *Blondie Chaplin*

Brian and Mike in the studio in the
Eighties.

GOOD VIBRATIONS
The Music

"I think our stuff has been guilty of being simplistic. Avant-garde,
  but simplistic. I think that eventually through interpretations
  like this being read by people who know or care or listen or feel
  the interpretation of what an artist felt at the time and what his
  surroundings were like, pretty soon it will be understood as some kind
  of folk art form that a group of guys from California who liked to sing
  all their lives got together and did."
Mike Love

"Being called a musical genius was a cross to bear. Genius is a big word.
  But if you have to live up to something, you might as well live up to
  that. Goddamn!"
Brian Wilson, *1988*

"Musically I am The Beach Boys."
Brian Wilson, *1988*

"We all just love harmonies so much. Harmonies are our main purpose.
  Messages are cool, but we've never been big on messages, obviously.
  The quality of clean vocals and little rhythmic trips against a very white
  track. We play very white music. We're probably the only group in
  America that does any more... Our purpose is just to be us. We're not
  trying to lay out too many heavy messages."
Al Jardine

"When I've thought out a theme I go to the piano and sit playing
  'feels', which are rhythm patterns and fragments of ideas. Then the
  song starts to blossom and become a real thing.

   "And all the while in the back of my mind I think about the
  limitations and capabilities of the boys. I never try the impossible, but
  I am always aware of the workable.

   "I respect everything I put on to disc. And I know for sure that
  The Beach Boys brought something new into rock 'n' roll."
Brian Wilson, *1966*

"The Beach Boys are lucky... we have a high range of voices. Mike can
  go from bass to the E above middle C, Dennis, Carl and Al progress
  upwards through C, A, and B. I can take the second D in the treble clef.
  The harmonies we were able to produce gave us a uniqueness which is
  really the only important thing you can put into records – some
  quality no one else has gotten into.

   "I know in some circles we're not regarded as that 'hip' or 'in'.
  This is maybe, because we haven't just arrived from nowhere with
  something new with a new label."
Brian Wilson, *1966*

"He (Brian) could have in his mind the four different parts...
He'd have four and five-part chords in his mind and he'd dish
them out to all of us. Then he'd take the top, which is the melody...
It never ceased to blow my mind that he could know those notes
and retain them."
Mike Love

"I've always been insecure about my lyrics. I always felt that what
I wanted to say was never imparted in my lyrics... that the message
just wasn't there."
Brian Wilson

"When I hear really fabulous material by other groups I feel as
small as the dot over the I in nit. Then I just have to create a new
song to bring me up on top.... That's probably my most compelling
motive for writing new songs – the urge to overcome an inferiority
feeling... I've never written one note or word of music simply
because I think it will make money. My ideas for the group are to
combine music that strikes a deep emotional response among listeners
and still maintains a some-what untrained and teenage sound.
I depend upon harmonics more than before and fuse it with a
1964-1965 approach in production."
Brian Wilson, *1965*

"I approach my music-making as an art-form – something
pure from the spirit to which I can add dynamics and marketable
reality. Music is genuine and healthy and the stimulation
I get from moulding it and adding dynamics is like nothing
else on earth."
Brian Wilson, *1966*

"When I come up with a new song that I'm excited about, I call
up the boys for a session. Sometimes I call them at the wrong time,
they're not in the mood to work and I have a hard time prying them
loose from their Hondas and chickies.
    "So finally we all agree on a date. It usually takes about three hours
to get everyone together in the studio. Once started we come on with
perfect teamwork.
    "We've established such rapport that we rarely need rehearsals.
They can read my mind, I read theirs, and we are as sensitive to each
other as seismographs. The boys don't usually hear my new songs until
we gather in the studio to record."
Brian Wilson, *1965*

"When I sit down at the piano and play a new song, the others
can visualize the whole arrangement right away. We take the melody
apart and work it out phrase by phrase. If they don't like my approach,
they suggest another. If Carl doesn't dig my idea, I'll change it
immediately because Carl has exquisite musical taste. I trust
it completely."
Brian Wilson, *1965*

"I suddenly realized that what is so great about the recording industry is that it is getting so free and intelligent that we can go into new things – string quartets, autoharps, instruments from another culture, dynamics."
Brian Wilson, *1966*

"Musically speaking all of us have become more creative. We used to be totally reliant on Brian but now we are branching out."
Mike Love, *1969*

"When you do something like *Pet Sounds,* they (the fans) expect you to keep going that way. I suppose *Pet Sounds* was our *Sgt. Pepper.* After that *Smiley Smile* was nothing more than a wild freak out, and *Wild Honey...* a trip in simplicity. Of all the many things that we've ever recorded *Good Vibrations* was one of the simplest that we've ever done. But the way it was conceived and put together gave the illusion of it being complex."
Carl Wilson, *1970*

"I think we're continuing with something we were three years too early with. I think the audience is just catching up to what we were trying to do with *Pet Sounds*. After *Smiley Smile* we had to sit back and mark time. We were getting too far ahead of the audience."
Bruce Johnston, *1971*

"Well, I feel I have something to say in music, in records. What I'm trying to get across is an attitude, a feeling about staying cool and all those little things in life that put you together. I'm just saying something about them, because I feel it's needed. You walk down around and see this grim stuff and it really makes you cry. And when you cry over something it means it got to you. Do you know what I mean."
Brian Wilson, *1976*

"I think a lot of the songs I have written and sung reflect my life. *I Just Wasn't Made For These Times* is very deep. *Surfer Girl, Caroline No, Till I Die, California Girls...* These songs have a lot of strength to them; they are very pretty and have deep meanings."
Brian Wilson, *1977*

"Carl mixes my stuff because I get too involved with every part. He's a good overall mixer... a great mixer. He can mix sixteen tracks because he has the feel for it. Brian lets him mix his stuff too. It's much more fun to hear what you're doing when somebody else is mixing it, because in the first place, I don't like all that sound coming down. It's not realistic."
Al Jardine

The Band

"God, my mom had to beat them to let me in the group. She said 'Come on, Brian, let him in or it'll break his heart! Mike and Brian went,'Nah, we don't want him'. But then Brian softened up, gave me a hug and, 'Aww, what the hell."
Dennis Wilson, *1977*

"You know, when The Beach Boys started, I wanted us to be a folk group. As it turns out, I feel that The Beach Boys became America's balladeers, recording in music the folk myths, the experience of this country."
Al Jardine

"The most important thing in our group venture is the kind of excitement we can create and express. When I'm excited about a new song, the boys catch it and we're off. We have a group spirit that won't stop."
Brian Wilson, *1965*

"I've been with The Beach Boys almost two years. I was in college when they were first formed and had their first local hit. New Year's Eve 1962 they played their first professional concert. The Wilsons are all from Hawthorne, which is a suburb about ten miles from Los Angeles.
   "Well, I became a manager at CBS and got to hear the first things The Beach Boys did. I thought they were so groovy, but after a year or so all of a sudden their harmony started expanding. I became a big fan. I have a fairly decent ear, so I got to know the chords and the parts and everything. One day Brian and the others were to go to NewOrleans to start a tour, but he was sick and couldn't go. So Mike Love phoned me to see if I could help him find a stand-in.
   "There was only an hour before his plane, and I phoned around everywhere I knew, but I couldn't find anyone. So Mike said, 'Why don't you come instead of Brian'."
Bruce Johnston *on how he became a Beach Boy*

"We can play harder rock than we've ever been able to play before. Ricky has been drumming since he was nine years old – he has more scope than Dennis who just maintained a steady hard beat for the vocals."
Mike Love *on Ricky Fataar, the session drummer who replaced Dennis for a while after he had injured his hand*

"I think you have to be constantly aware of the teenagers, because after all we are a young group of kids, so we should still be making music for the kids. I see no reason to desert them, you know what I mean?"
Brian Wilson

"Dennis was the best surfer and he was the one who really had the idea for the band."
Carl Wilson

"Carl is R&B. He keeps the group in tune with rhythm and blues music. Dennis, I would consider him hitting the twenty-five to thirty-five bracket. Al Jardine is also like Mike Love – he sounds young. So Al and Mike are responsible for the youth, Carl and Dennis are recognisable for twenty-five to thirty-five and I think I'm responsible for the twenty-five to forty-five. So it's a careful blend of age groups we hit."
Brian Wilson

"We're a well co-ordinated team trying to put that little extra that's new and different into the world of pop music... our world."
Brian Wilson, *1966*

"Brian Wilson is The Beach Boys. He is the band. We're his fucking messengers. He is all of it. Period. We're nothing. He's everything."
Dennis Wilson

"No, we are not just Brian's puppets. Brian plays the major creative role in the production of our music, but everyone in the group contributes something to the finished product. It's not like an orchestra translating the wishes of the conductor. We all have a part to play in the production of the records.
  "Brian works out the basic arrangement before we ever go into the studio. We run through it a few times and there are often suggestions made about changes or improvements. Everybody contributes ideas. We all give something, although I agree that Brian contributes the major part."
Carl Wilson

"I suddenly realized that The Beach Boys weren't giving the young people exactly what they wanted. While Lennon and McCartney were exciting everyone with their new sounds, we were static. That's why I concentrated on giving the group a sound that would have lasting appeal."
Brian Wilson, *1966*

"I see them as a group of young men who have made a lot of money, but who have had to earn that money, who have had to work hard and have known hardships. I don't know if we'll keep the money, you just don't know what's going to happen. I see them as a sensibly, efficiently clean-cut group, without being male equivalents of Doris Day."
Bruce Johnston, *1967*

"After we'd pretty well established ourselves and created a situation where we could relax and really dig into different musical directions, I suppose I had a string of ambitions, coinciding with each new venture into a new form of music. Every once in a while, an individual is born into the world whose whole being is music. I think Brian is one of those rare people. It was a blow to us when he decided not to tour with the group any longer, but he needed time to work on his writing and the tour schedules were heavy."
Carl Wilson, *1969*

"We've been fighting this antiquated image for longer than I can remember. Because of the attitude of a few mental dinosaurs intent on exploiting our initial success, Brian's huge talent has never been fully appreciated in America and the potential of the group has been stifled.

"It's only now with our own operation that we are beginning to be appreciated on a different level.

"If The Beatles had suffered this kind of misrepresentation, they would never have got past singing *Please Please Me* and *I Wanna Hold Your Hand* and leaping around in Beatle suits."
Dennis Wilson, *1970*

"Recently people have rediscovered us. In New York they've been calling us 'Beach'. Just 'Beach', like a very hip term."
Bruce Johnston, *1971*

"The Beach Boys are not a superstar group. The music is the superstar of the group."
Dennis Wilson

"I was a hermit. I was a musical hermit and I did stay alone. It's all true that I did have a sandbox in my house. It was the size of one room and we had a piano in the sand. The story about staying home and writing in the sandbox is all true, and is pretty close to how I really am.

"The mystique grew, and I was getting fascinated with the fact that I was becoming famous and that there was an interest in my style of life, you know, a very eccentric person, and people began taking note of that."
Brian Wilson, *1976*

"We'll always have a public. The Beach Boys are inseparable from the white middle-class karma."
Mike Love, *1976*

"They just hired some musicians to play in the background and I did *Back Home* and *Love Is A Woman* from the new album. I did *Good Vibrations* too. My doctor at the time thought I should do it, so I did it. I enjoyed it. Yes, very much. The others, my brothers that is, they liked it a lot too."
Brian Wilson *on his appearance on 'Saturday Night Live', 1977*

"It was a bit like eight years in graduate school, part of my musical way of growing up. It taught me how to do what I do now. I became a spoke in a very successful wheel and eventually it turned into a sort of legacy for me – financing me to do what I do now."
Bruce Johnston, *1977*

"All I know is he got into a terrible fight with Jack Rieley. Some dispute, and they got into a terrible fight, and the next day Bruce was gone."
Brian Wilson *on the departure of Bruce Johnston, 1972*

"We had a meeting and we discussed the personal problems within the group, and the relationships between the various members within the group. Some of us had no relationship at all, and Bruce said, 'If that's the way you feel about it, maybe I should just leave – I don't want to leave, but maybe it's for the best...' He had his own interests, his own relationships with the press, and he played a game that was oblique to The Beach Boys. But now he's free to do what he pleases. The Beach Boys never threw Bruce out, he was just on a tangent that was outside The Beach Boys for so many years."
Mike Love *on Bruce Johnston's departure*

"Bruce's future... it's all based on individual musical taste and individual aspirations, which are fine, but not within the framework of a group... His lifestyle is changing like everyone else's... We're still friends."
Mike Love *on Bruce Johnston's departure*

"I wasn't feeling comfortable or having a good time any more. I thought it better to leave when I did and stay friends with everybody than leave two years later and be enemies.
  "I had to leave when I did because I felt isolated in terms of studio development. The obvious thing would have been to do my own solo album straight after quitting, but things just didn't work that way."
Bruce Johnston *explains his departure, 1977*

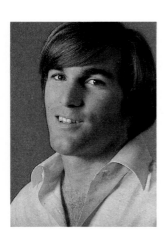

"To me, *Surf's Up* is, and always has been, one hyped up lie! It was a false reflection of The Beach Boys, and one which Jack (Rieley) engineered right from the outset. Jack was just very, very smart in that he was able to camouflage what was actually going on by making it look like Brian Wilson was more than just a visitor at those sessions. Jack made it appear as though Brian was really there all the time."
Bruce Johnston *on the fight that caused him to leave The Beach Boys*

"We were more concerned with Brian's return to the group. Every day he just gets better and better – more so when he's in the studio. And that's all that matters.
  "He's lost weight, he's healthy again and working well. I suppose a sign of any artist's true greatness is when, against all odds, they make a successful comeback.

"I'll be truthful with you. There were many times when I'd
look at my brother and think to myself, maybe he won't ever pull
it together again. He went through a lot of bad times. Drugs
didn't help.

"If we had lost Brian, I guess we'd have had to go on without
him but we always felt in our hearts that things would turn out
the way they have and we were prepared to wait and wait.

"But there were other things as well. Michael and his
meditation... there were our divorces... Carl fighting the
draft board... so many things can come down at the same time,
and they did. Also, when it came to the matter of business affairs,
I have to admit The Beach Boys weren't the smartest guys
around."
Dennis Wilson, *1977*

"I can tell you the day The Beach Boys will no longer exist - never.
We'll be on stage in wheelchairs."
Dennis Wilson, *1977*

"The main trip is music for sure. Brian was always more
into music as a vibration, a sound feeling and vibration, right?
More than lyrics or anything words could ever say. And it's
really true. Music, a really heavy vibration, says a lot more
than a million words could say. As far as really holy sounds go."
Carl Wilson

"In the past we all used to have our own representatives at
a board meeting and the group would be outnumbered by lawyers
and accountants. When the key to your music is harmony and
the harmony among you is constantly under attack, your music
suffers tremendously."
Carl Wilson, *1980*

"Business. The personal we've sacrificed a little bit in order to
keep business going. We're doing it for the furtherment of the
group's popularity and institutionalisation. And we're sacrificing
some, 'Hello there, how are you?' and all that stuff."
Brian Wilson *asked about the relationships in the band,* *1988*

"They (Beach Boys) got stumbling along this career as
background singers. Not stumbling along , but moving along.
Like going faster than they could actually run. Everyone was
so tuned into the sound we were making that there was no
problem with it."
Brian Wilson, *1988*

"The Beach Boys went from being a little stand-up bass/
wire brush/one guitar group all the way to a giant institution
of American pop music. We're all proud of that. But none of
us get along."
Brian Wilson, *1988*

Transcendental Meditation

"The Maharishi's ideas are so simple and so right that I cannot begin
to explain how impressed I was. I know he realises we will publicise his
ideas but that does not deface them. He wants to spread the beliefs."
Mike Love, *1967*

"We met the Maharishi Mahesh Yogi in December 1967 when we
did a United Nations show in Paris. The whole group now meditates.
Al and I are teachers. Any group is only as strong as its members.
I don't think I'd be in the group if it wasn't for meditation.
It raises your tolerance to tension and stress. It helps against the
fatiguing effects of physical and mental activity."
Mike Love, *1978*

"I meditate, and also I think about meditation, which is funny.
I think that's gonna be the answer. As it progresses, I think that I'm
going to gather more peace of mind, I'll be able to gather my thoughts
a little easier. I think it's going to aid my creativity."
Brian Wilson

"All of a sudden I felt this weirdness, this presence this guy had. Like out of left field. First thing he ever said to me (was) 'Live your life to the fullest'. So the next day I went over to his room, and he said, 'Tell me some words of your songs'. So we told him the lyrics to *God Only Knows* and he goes, 'That's the sun rising and the stars and the planets and it connects with... 'So I said, 'God, this is great!' And he said, 'We'd like to initiate you into the programme'."
Dennis Wilson *on meeting the Maharishi Mahesh Yogi for the first time, 1968*

"It's (TM) a very personal, fulfilling thing. It stimulates the mind and body and gives you a greater appreciation of life. It puts you in communication with something infinitely greater and more important than self."
Dennis Wilson

"Maharishi, he's really fantastic to be with. Every time I've been with him I've felt very good. He's a very spontaneous person. How happy he is, and things like his laugh are very contagious. And very powerful.

"We were in Paris, doing a UNICEF show, and we met Maharishi there. We talked to him for several hours, and we were all initiated. I meditate regularly. It's helped me to cope with things. Things affect me less. Bad things affect me less- pardon me, I would rather say difficult things. I find that it relaxes me very deeply and gives me energy. I recommend it highly."
Carl Wilson

"When I heard about TM I consciously took steps to expand my awareness... I didn't want to live my life at the same level twenty years from now... And one of the greatest things that interested me was that (the Maharishi) said, 'You don't have to give up your Rolls-Royce... and forsake all your pursuits of material pleasures... to develop inner spiritual qualities'. That sounded real good to me."
Mike Love, *1968*

"It (TM) gives me a chance to see a side of life I don't see often. But I sit down in a chair; I don't fold my legs like a yogi, because my legs are too big 'cause I'm out of shape. So jeese, it's a big pain."
Brian Wilson, *1976*

"To me, religion is communicating with yourself. Some people call it Universal Consciousness, others God, there are so many different terms. It goes down to the innermost part of yourself, really. From what I've seen, a lot of religion is forced on people and you can't have things forced on you. People in the States are told to go to church on Sunday and they resent it. But of course, you don't have to go to church to be religious – you don't need to go anywhere to be religious. With some people it's finding peace with themselves to begin with. Subconsciously, I'm very religious."
Carl Wilson

Wisdom, Philosophy & Witlessness

"The feeling we create is love."
Brian Wilson, *1988*

"We're still there. If there was no media we'd still be doing it.
We're still the same group, same people, same ideas, same everything.
A little older. The Beach Boys just reported and sang about what was
going on for them, what was so for us. I think we represent to people
in other countries, and even in America, something that they imagine
that we do. Everyone has fantasies. People use The Beach Boys for their
thoughts of America, or what America should be, or the beach.
The Beach Boys created a safe place for people. Even though I was in the
band, I could lie in bed at night and listen to the radio, the lights out,
and *In My Room* would come on and I'd get into it. A place for
people to let go and kind of drift, to enjoy themselves."
Dennis Wilson

"I'm sure The Beach Boys are viewed as an institution,
but the main reason for our popularity has to be the songs."
Brian Wilson, *1977*

"The philosophy of the band is that we don't want to play stadiums
or be No.1 on the charts – although we do want to be No.0, infinity,
to be known for centuries. But we only want to play for people or causes
that are the most uplifting."
Mike Love

"The problem with popularity is that if it gets too popular everybody
leaves and goes somewhere else."
Mike Love, *1975*

"There will always be a Beach Boys. Being a Beach Boy is like
being in love."
Dennis Wilson, *1976*

"I'd swop a lot of The Beach Boys' songs for just one *Michelle*."
Bruce Johnston

"My own name, Love, fits me. I'm mentally mature but emotionally
a high-school boy still."
Mike Love

"I'm not a genius. I'm just a hard working guy."
Brian Wilson

"The public thinks of us as surfing Doris Days."
Bruce Johnston

"What holds us together as a team now is music... and greed.
No... no. I don't really mean that. But I would like to convey that despite
the songs of surf, fun and girls we are not innocuous people."
Mike Love

"We've had some problems as individuals. But as a group, we're very blessed and very fortunate to defy time and all kinds of reason and continue to put out those good vibrations."
Mike Love, *1984*

"They depend on me a lot, come to think about it. They couldn't function without me – they'd flounder. I believe that what I'm doing is creating things for them. I do it for the group. Everything I do is for the group."
Brian Wilson

"I love my old friend, music, it's my best friend. It's hard to explain how much music can mean to some people. It's a dear friend, but it's like wearing the same t-shirt every day."
Carl Wilson, *1971*

"You're called a genius by people, and then your whole life you become the part."
Brian Wilson, *1988*

"If there wasn't The Beach Boys and there wasn't music, I would not even talk to them. But through the music I fell in love with my brothers."
Dennis Wilson

"Maybe I have a genius for arrangements and harmonics, but I don't think I am a genius. I believe the word genius applies only to people who can do things that other people can't do. I can't do things others can't. I wasn't a genius in high school and I'm not now."
Brian Wilson

"I believe The Beatles will re-form, and they'll play with The Beach Boys. That will be great."
Brian Wilson, *1980*

"We've done everything together. Shit, eat, fart, cry, laugh. Everything."
Dennis Wilson

"I'd like to donate everything I make and do to the environment and ecology. I'd like to get a list of them. We've been thinking and talking about it but I'm tired of just talking. I wanna do free shows, get rid of the pollutant in the cock, in the mind, everywhere. From syphilis to smog. I really honestly want to do something about it. I have an idea. If every group would donate one record, one album, absolutely all the publishing and all the writer's royalties – everything to the cause of ecology that'd really help out. Three shows per year, 100% of the money. And every record company, for a tax write-off, would donate a certain amount to ecology or to a free clinic or to mental health."
Dennis Wilson

"In the last two years all I ever cut, all I ever recorded, was skimpy
little bits and pieces; little fragments. Something happened to my
concentration – I don't exactly know what, but it weakened for some
reason – and I lost the ability to concentrate enough to follow through.
But that's my own problem; because of hang-ups I have.

"I get too mental; and I don't think I follow my instincts as much as
I should. I used to – shit, for years in a row! I mean 'instinct', I used to
think up them hits one after the other. Then I got too thoughtful about
it and fucked up. So I suppose I have to get back on my fucking feet and
trust my instincts and go with them a little while.

"There's a lotta different ways to go. One way is very 'mental', trusting
in your mind; the second is kinda going with your 'instincts', and the
third would be force. If the first two fail, the last sets in – but that can
work too.

"Eight years with no hits. Eight years without something the kids'll buy
on instinct!"
Brian Wilson, *1976*

"I find empathy for a subject through communication with people.
For instance, I have never surfed but my brother Dennis is an excellent
surfer and I experience the thrill of riding a wave with him."
Brian Wilson, *1966*

"With *Good Vibrations* it got into a space of more like we're looking
for the inner values in people, the inner values in life, not so subtle
because really the inner is the basis of the outer, so we were picking
up on the good vibrations, being more sensitive where people are
coming from, you know, so that showed a change and growth, an
awareness in the group that led into the next phase in our career, which
in some ways was less dramatic in terms of overall popularity, but it was
tremendously equally dramatic in terms of uniqueness and innovation,
and like the *Smiley Smile* album and all that, they are tremendously
unique albums and very avant-garde and everything,
so much so that we lost a lot of people on the way."
Mike Love

"Making an album is an excursion into creativity. No real true
loopholes or things standing in the way when you get into creativity.
Creativity cuts a hole right in glass. It can cut through glass, it can cut
through steel. Nothing stops creativity. The creative urge in mankind is
somewhere way up on the totem pole of experience. Some people might
think that sex is the highest experience you can have. I tend to think
that music is."
Brian Wilson, *1988*

"Most of my dreams are about money, cars and girls... Three of us are
brothers and we naturally get into some pretty good scraps which blow
over soon. There's no chance of The Beach Boys coming unglued,
however... They tell me I'm the guy with the quick temper and far-out
temperament."
Dennis Wilson, *1965*

In 1980, The Beach Boys were inducted into the Rock 'n' Roll Hall of Fame. During their acceptance speech, Mike Love shocked everyone with a public denunciation of practically every celebrity present:

"Billy Joel was an opening act for The Beach Boys in the '60s, and when we did our 25th anniversary special, I tried to get him to say a few words – because one of the first dates he had with Christie Brinkley was to bring her out to a Beach Boys' concert. She was taking photos and he got up on stage, like the big man he is, he was playing the piano on *Barbara Ann* and a couple of others, and I thought it would be pretty cool to have Billy Joel say something about how his first date, like a lot of other people, was at a Beach Boys' show and then go into 'Barbara Ann'. So I tried to get that done, and he wouldn't respond – 'cos I guess he was 'too cool' or something – so as a consequence, I think that's really disgusting, that a person gets too big to remember when he was an opening act for The Beach Boys. I think that's getting too ego'ed out, too unapproachable.

"The same goes for Mick Jagger. I said he was chickenshit to get on the stage with The Beach Boys. Because Mick Jagger is very clever, and he doesn't want to get a band like The Beach Boys doing 35 smash hits before he goes on stage, because it would put a serious hurt on his career. And I said that, I said Mick Jagger was chickenshit to get on stage with The Beach Boys, in so many words; and I mean it sincerely! There's no unity in the music business.

"The point of my messages that night was that there's all these things going on all the time all over the world, whether it's starvation or destruction of the planet, or whatever, which could probably be helped by a body of concerned citizens in the music business. But they're not, they're all divided; their egos divide them, their agencies divide them, their attorneys divide them, their record companies are cheating everybody left, right and centre – there's not a whole lot of sweetness and light coming from that whole end of things. So my remarks that night were meant to shock, and to say that it would be great if the music business stood for something other than all this ego, divisiveness, greed and corruption. Not that it will change anything, it was just me expressing my viewpoint."
Mike Love *looking back on Rock'n'Roll Hall Of Fame induction, 1993*

"There's a fire burning inside a youth's body. It's the fire of youth. I call it the '20's people'. It's a boundless competitive urge; a crazy, fucked up feeling that tells you you've got to get out there and do it. You got to stay up with the Joneses. You've got to win. You can't be called a loser. If it gets too heavy, the kids drop out and the men go ahead. The loser people drop out and the winner people keep going. When my name comes up, I just want people to say 'winner'."
Brian Wilson, *1988*

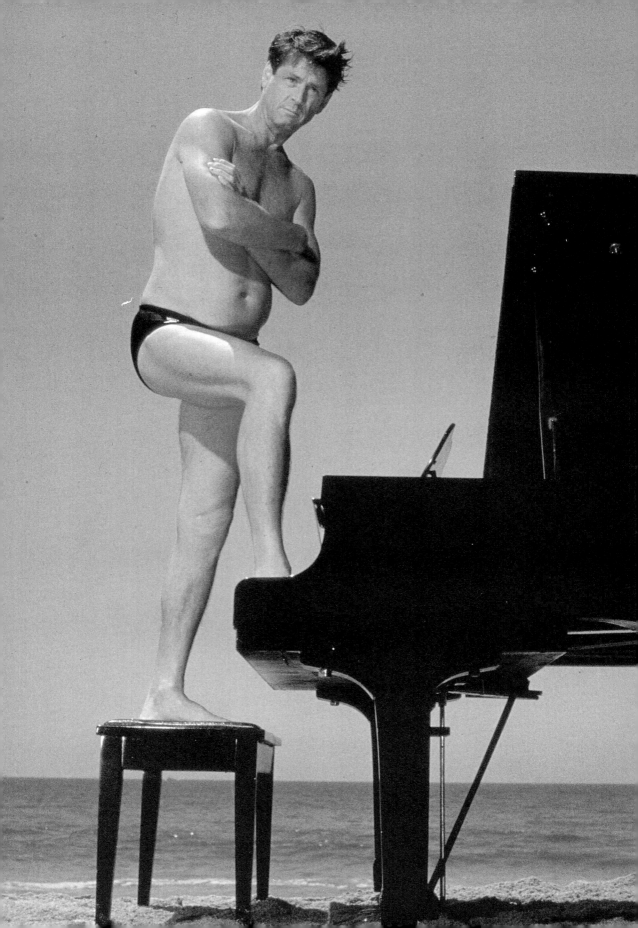

SURF MUSIC & ITS IMAGE

"The ocean scares me."
Brian Wilson, *1976*

"When a new fad comes along we'll be the first to ride it."
Brian Wilson, *1965*

"We aim to keep up with what young guys and dolls are doing and thinking. It doesn't have to be specifically about surfing, hot rodding or motor scooting. We can't be too dedicated to current crazes because the pressure builds up on us to follow through until they die – and we with 'em."
Brian Wilson, *1965*

"Success took us out of the surf. We rarely get a chance to ride the wild waves now. The good old summertime, the best surfing months, is our busiest season on tour."
Dennis Wilson, *1965*

"We blew that part of our image. When the surf's up we are likely to be in bone-dry, Kansas, soaking in perspiration or wetting our hides under the showers."
Brian Wilson, *1965*

"Now you don't see so many surfing and hot rod albums. Today it's the Honda scene. You've got to be on the motor scooter kick to be really 'in'. Those baby motor bikes are really thrifty. You can drive all over town for a week on thirty cents."
Brian Wilson, *1965*

"There was a time when it was uncool to be into The Beach Boys, and when we did that album *Summer Days (And Summer Nights)* it started to bother us, doing this same stuff, because we thought we were trapped into having to sing about a certain thing."
Carl Wilson

"We came on very big in the surf days. It was just beginning to become a popular sport and our songs came right in as a vehicle to its rising general appeal. Then we sank into a severe depression. Our discs were still selling but somehow our image faded away. Now we seem to be getting back on our feet. Guys no longer drive around with surf boards on their cars when they're a hundred miles from water – which is an indication of tastes in music becoming more and more sophisticated."
Carl Wilson, *1968*

"It's not a matter of us changing our name. People have to be
re-educated."
Al Jardine

"The trouble in the past has been due to the fact that Capitol
insisted on trying to push our old image. When we put out *Pet Sounds*
they were really worried. This was one of the reasons we decided to form
our own company. I know it's a pretty far out statement to make, but
we're never gonna put out any old product just for the sake of
selling records."
Carl Wilson, *1970*

"We figured there were a million people on the planet who didn't
know about *Good Vibrations* and the *Pet Sounds* album, but thought
we just sang about surf boards. So we developed a real complex about it.
It's been a stigma and we went through a period of trying to get away
from it. Now we have convinced enough people we are on to other
music as well, we can afford to go back and sing about surfing."
Al Jardine, *1970*

"They were against *Pet Sounds* and all the albums that came after.
They wanted us to stick with surfin' and hot rod records, you know.
But we said, well you know, we don't want to do that. We're doing
other music now. But they really weren't going for it. And so they
had all these hundreds of people in their organisation pushing
another thing. People were bound to get the wrong impression
about the group."
Carl Wilson, *1970*

"Surfing music is dead. It was just a summer craze for kids on the beach.
I'm finished with it."
Brian Wilson

"I was into carburettors, cars, peeling out, cruising, A/W root beers,
I was 'into' root beer; I was also into tit, nipples, dirty pictures – I loved
dirty pictures, magazines, Tijuana, surfboards on top of the car.
Even if I wasn't going surfing on that day, I'd put em' up there anyway.
Anything to do with that – with having fun."
Dennis Wilson, *1971*

"He wanted a sandbox, so he got a sandbox. I mean, who am I to tell a
creator what he can do? He said 'I want to play in the sand, I want to feel
like a little kid. When I'm writing these songs I want to feel what I'm
writing, all the happiness.
 "So he had this really good carpenter come up to the house, and
in the dining room ,the guy built a gorgeous wood sandbox, around
two and a half feet tall. And they came with a dump truck and dumped
eight tons of sand in it. And the sand, being that there is no sun,
is freezing cold. By the way, the dogs had also used it - you know,
dogs and sand."
Marilyn Wilson *on Brian's attempt at rejuvenation*

"I tried it a couple of times, a long time ago, but I never was a good surfer. I could never, you know, do it very well."
Carl Wilson, *1975 (Dennis was the only good surfer in the band)*

"In those days we were writing about what we knew – high schools, going to the beach and surfing. After we'd been around the world and seen many other facets of our life our ideas deepened, but I think the songs came just as easily."
Mike Love, *1975*

"We grew up in that Southern California environment. It was a very specialised jargon and way of not only talking but looking and dressing and acting and there were different groups and one was the surfers and the other was the hoods or the greasers or whatever you call them. We identified more with the athletic, you know surfers, good time cruisers rather than the real heavy other type of thing."
Mike Love, *1975*

"It has probably changed a lot since then. I'm not really into it now. It was just life, you know. It was just what was happening."
Carl Wilson *on the 'beach scene', 1975*

"I don't know why everybody doesn't live at the beach, on the ocean. It makes no sense to me, hanging around the dirty, ugly-as-shit city. That's why I always loved and was proud to be a Beach Boy; I always loved the image. On the beach, you can live in bliss."
Dennis Wilson, *1976*

"I hate those old falsettos, I really do, and it's embarrassing since I've grown up. They just packaged them and I guess they've sold better than anything we've done in a while. We grew up with it, we were a product of all that. There was surfing and California girls and cars, that was California. I don't relate to that, the whole California thing, any more."
Brian Wilson *on the repackaged* Endless Summer *album and other reissues, 1976*

ON & OFF THE ROAD

"For three straight years we've been hearing the screaming of live audiences and we've grown dependent on that sound. Believe me, nothing is better for the ego. Maybe it's too good for the ego. We live by it."
Brian Wilson, *1965*

"Like some animals are super-sensitive to the weather, we are sensitive to the moods of the crowds. As soon as we enter an auditorium we can tell what type of a crowd we'll have. There's either a chilling silence or a mild roar even before the show starts."
Carl Wilson, *1965*

"Nobody knew what was going on. I wouldn't even look at anyone. That night the road manager took me back to LA and I didn't want to see anybody except my mother."
Brian Wilson *on the nervous breakdown that caused him to quit touring altogether*

"I told them I foresaw a beautiful future for The Beach Boys, but the only way we could achieve it was if they did their job and I did mine. They would have to get a replacement for me."
Brian Wilson *on quitting touring and telling the band*

"Mike lost his cool and felt like there was no reason to go on. Dennis picked up a big ashtray and told some people to get out of there or he'd hit them in the head with it. He kind of blew it, you know.
"Al Jardine broke out in tears and had stomach cramps. He was all goofed up, and my mother who was there, had to take care of him.

"And good old Carl was the only guy who never got into a bad emotional scene. He just sat there and didn't get uptight about it. He always kept a cool head. If it wasn't for Carl, it's hard to say where we would be. He was the greatest stabilising influence in the group.... He cooled Dennis, Mike, and Al down."
Brian Wilson *recalling the reaction after telling the band he would not tour again*

"You know the idea of a show with The Beach Boys and The Mamas and The Papas is okay. But all those people from England who play acid rock – if the audience is coming to see them, they're going to hate us."
Brian Wilson *offering a reason why The Beach Boys didn't show up at the Monterey Pop Festival*

"Brian was on the board, and it changed several times, the concept of it. And he decided, 'Well shit, let's not play it'. And I think there were some people getting hostile about the group at the time, you know, about the surfing thing. And he figured, 'Fuck you, or something like that', I don't know. I'm really glad the way things have turned out. I'm really grateful, actually, the way everything has happened.
   "The most important thing was that we had a chance to sort of cool out and develop, you know? That was necessary for the group to really carry on and do anything. 'Cause you could make hits all week long, but it just wouldn't mean shit. As far as making good music, you need time, I mean some of us do. Brian advanced way beyond the rest of the group, and we really had to start to catch up."
Carl Wilson *on the cancellation of The Beach Boys' appearance at the Monterey Pop Festival*

"Brian is happy at home; that's the way he likes it. But the rest of us really enjoy travelling around. No it's not that we have to, we're not doing it because somebody's got to. We like meeting people, we like making music in public."
Carl Wilson

"We toured in March, April, May – if we go and do a summer tour, which we're likely to do and a winter tour, it probably adds up to over 100 consecutive days performing on stage. Then we spend a good couple of months recording, then there are the photo sessions. Being a Beach Boy consumes an awful lot of time, an awful lot of energy. In between, we're tired and we rest, that's how it's been."
Mike Love, *1966*

"More than anything, I miss singing with the guys... I have that falsetto that I guess I could capitalize on. I love singing. I sing in the shower all the time. I sing alone and I think, 'Wow, if I only had a microphone here!'."
Brian Wilson

"It felt good to get up there again. When I first got up on stage I felt a little self-conscious... So I thought, 'Okay, I'm going to have some fun'. But on the second night I started to feel dizzy from the amps."
Brian Wilson *on his return to the stage, 1970*

"We had a lawsuit with Capitol and decided to go – go outside, like to Europe and Czechoslovakia... It's real bleak black there; not very much freedom but one of the most tumultuous audiences we've ever had was in Prague."
Bruce Johnston

"If it was for free, ok. But to keep doing it for money – I don't think I dig robbing from children. The best thing they've done in the last 10 years was that Pakistani concert, the one George Harrison did in Madison Square Garden. But I don't feel comfortable making money that way, it's out of all proportion what the big groups are charging. The kids can't afford it."
Brian Wilson, *1971*

"We toured and we'd go up there and do the hits. Like 45 minutes, all the records, one after the other, just like a 'live' juke-box. That was all it was. And the fans were real loud, a lot of girls screaming and yelling and stuff – it was fun, but I dig playing a lot more now that we do so much more on stage."
Carl Wilson

"We do not under any circumstances play the old songs except in encores. And we don't wear striped shirts like we once did."
Bruce Johnston, *1971*

"I like to see a group or person entertain me... that's why I wear my gold lamé jacket and turban. Even though Carl dresses pretty spiffy too, the rest of the group doesn't care so much. Of course, just because Al Jardine hasn't changed his underwear since the Japan tour in sixty-five – I mean you can't ask for everything."
Mike Love

"I feel more into it... Rehearsals went real good. I got some of the old fire back and I feel more positive. I feel good about myself, and once you feel good about yourself you can touch other people. I lost weight and acquired self-discipline... I wanted to be a full band member again... In the early days I would also play bass... the period of adjustment wasn't as traumatic as some people think."
Brian Wilson *on his return to the stage*

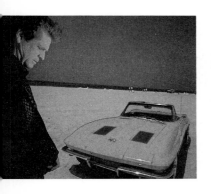

"It's really a treat to have all five of us back on the road playing together. With Brian back it isn't a chore any more."
Dennis Wilson, *1977*

"If I said we could reproduce that record sound on stage I'd be nuts. We get the occasional comments from people who say we don't sound like the records. But it's not a dumb comment to make because naturally we're not like the records. It's people who usually don't pay to come in and see the show who criticise."
Mike Love

"I do feel more like a member now again. It's a little easier to
cope now. I played about 35 shows last year. It was a little scary to
be out there, but it was very productive, and the group worked hard
together, and I was just thrilled to be part of it.
"The group's very positive about it. They act a lot more positive than
they ever have before, especially about doing tours and everything like
that. The boys believe in themselves, they believe they have something
good to offer people and they're doing their job."
Brian Wilson, *1977*

"I only went out on tour because my psychiatrist said I should get back
into circulation. It was a worthwhile experience. Although I wouldn't say
I enjoyed it, it was interesting. At first I was scared, but eventually got
used to going out there and calmed down a bit."
Brian Wilson, *on his motive for resuming touring***,** *1977*

"I didn't ever think I would be back touring with The Beach Boys again.
They asked me to do it and I said OK. It's like racketball, you make a
commitment once you get on the court. The other guy serves and you
have to play."
Brian Wilson, *1977*

"Touring is the greatest way of life. The other day I thought – what
would it be like to go on a sixty day tour? I came to the conclusion that
I'd prefer that to living at home."
Brian Wilson, *1980*

Oldies Band

"A lot of kids coming to see us now weren't even born when the first surfing hits were recorded in 1961. For a long time we refused to sing stuff like *Surfin' USA*. But finally we realised that we were revisiting our own history. Now we've learnt to embrace our past."
Carl Wilson, *1977*

"On the new tour that's coming up we will be doing the new stuff as well as some old material. There will always be people wanting to hear the older tunes. I don't get bored with them... they're fun."
Dennis Wilson

"We have ended up in a time-warp, the music seems to keep renewing itself. To me it feels very much the same as when I first started."
Carl Wilson, *1980*

"So finally it's 1976 and we're still riding on our past success. I mean, I've gone on like that for I don't know how long."
Brian Wilson

"They were denying that whole success period. They were going through a rebellious period and they were actually denying the songs that made them famous, but then they got back into what I call being proud of one's thing, and I think it's working better for them now. They got very arty and they thought maybe they didn't have to carry that with them. But any artist should know that you carry along that which made you famous when you do your show."
Brian Wilson, *1976*

"It's all part of the same thing... our roots go right back to *Surfin'* and we don't try to disassociate ourselves from our past. I'm honoured by our achievements and proud to still be around, so ultimately it doesn't really matter if the public bought more copies of *20 Golden Greats* than *15 Big Ones*. The one thing that they all had in common was that they were buying The Beach Boys."
Dennis Wilson, *1977*

"I was talking to Brian the other day about the fact that the band hasn't released a new record in a long while and he said, 'Well, good things take time'."
Dennis Wilson, *1976*

BAD VIBRATIONS
Drugs

"I have a very bright mind and this LSD will really expand my mind and make me write better."
Brian Wilson *contemplating using LSD*

"I saw God and it just blew my mind. My mind was blown."
Brian Wilson *after his first acid trip, 1965*

"About a year ago I had what I consider a very religious experience. I took LSD, a full dose of LSD, and later, another time, I took a smaller dose. And I learned a lot of things like patience, understanding. I can't teach you or tell you what I learned from taking it. But I consider it a very religious experience."
Brian Wilson, *1966*

"I told him... we were driving to a recording session, and I said, 'I heard that you experimented with LSD. Is that a put-on to the newspaper, or did you do it?' And he said, 'Yes, dad, I did',and I said 'Well Brian, do you think you're strong enough in your brain that you can experiment with a chemical that might drive you crazy later?' He says, 'No, dad, it's opened a lot of things for me'. And I said, 'Brian, who are you trying to kid?' He said, 'Well, I had weird, weird hallucinations, it made me understand'. And I said, 'Who you trying to kid, Brian? What did you understand, except seeing a bunch of different nightmares in your brain, colours and things like that?' And he agreed that he'd never do it again. And I said, 'You know, Brian, one thing God gives you is a brain, if you play with it and destroy it, you're dead, you're a vegetable. And we haven't heard the rest of this, there are going to be a lot of people killed and people in asylums, because they played, you know, because they played with God.

   "If you want to print it, I would be happy to have you do it. These guys that have to be freaked out on marijuana and other things on stage to become artists, should never have the privilege of stepping onto a stage to play for young impressionable people."
Murry Wilson

"I was working with Van Dyke Parks, he and I both took drugs to
work together and it worked to the positive."
Brian Wilson, *1976*

"Acid showed me a combination of sounds – how to combine
different instruments to get a sound there's no instrument for.
Infinite sounds. Forever sounds. Sounds that are combined and
echoed so they remind you of something you can't touch. I started
thinking about sounds and that's where *Pet Sounds* came from.
Acid also taught me about colour and showed me that it's more
vivid than I ever imagined."
Brian Wilson

"We went ahead and lay on the floor recording with the microphones
about a foot from the ground. We were so stoned we had to lie down.
We got to the point where we thought this was the way to record.
We got halfway through the album before we decided to stand up
because we got sleepy."
Brian Wilson *recalling the* Smile *sessions*

"Michael, I know all about drug abuse. I abuse drugs, I do not
condone them."
**Carl Wilson *to Mike Love defending his brother Dennis'
drug antics***

"In Fort Worth, Texas, there is a drug clinic which takes people
off the streets and helps them get over bad LSD trips. They don't use
any traditional medical treatment whatsoever. All they do is play the
patient our *Smiley Smile* album and apparently this acts as a soothing
remedy which relaxes them and helps them to recover completely
from their trip."
Carl Wilson, *1970*

"I always appreciated the musical changes. The only thing that
I didn't like about that period was that those guys hanging around
Brian at that time were into a lot of drugs, and I didn't appreciate
or dig that. And so I may have projected a little bit of, if not animosity,
then something resembling it, towards people who would just come
by and hang out with Brian and try to get him high and give him
drugs."
Mike Love *on the* Pet Sounds *era*

"I was taking a lot of cocaine, a lot of uppers, and I got my life
all fucked up. They got me into such a paranoid state that I'd snort
cocaine in my room and then it got to the point where I liked it there.
Then pretty soon, I didn't like it any more, but I had no choice,
because I'd gotten into the pattern of staying in my room. I wasn't
able to create because of the drugs. At first, I was creative on drugs
and then I got to a point where I couldn't even go to the piano –
I was too afraid."
Brian Wilson

"Up until four months ago I was taking a lot of cocaine. And these doctors
came in and showed me a way to stop doing it, which is having bodyguards
with you all the time so you can't get to it... That approach works because
there's someone right there all the time... It keeps you on the spot.
They catch you when you're ready to do something you shouldn't do. It
works until you have finally reached the stage you don't need it any more.

   "It doesn't quite end with that simplistic, and somewhat 'cold turkey'
style of cure. They teach me socialization, how to socialize. They're just
teaching me different social graces, like manners... (I did have them),
but I lost them. Drugs took 'em away... I got real paranoid, I couldn't
do anything.

   "I was unhappy as all heck. I knew I was screwing myself up, and
I couldn't do anything about it. I was a useless little vegetable. I made
everybody very angry at me because I wasn't able to work, to get off my
butt. Coke every day. Goin' over to parties. Just having bags of snow
around, just snortin' it down like crazy."
Brian Wilson, *1976*

"The way I deal with it is I go jogging in the morning. I goddamn get
out of bed and I jog, and I make sure I stay in shape. That's how I do it.
And so far the only way I've been keeping from drugs is with those
bodyguards, and the only way I've been going jogging is those
bodyguards have been taking me jogging."
Brian Wilson, *1976*

"Dennis had been hanging around and he got Brian to buy maybe
fifteen thousand dollars' worth of cocaine. Brian would snort up five
or six grand in a half an hour, and they'd have to put their hands in his
mouth to stop him from swallowing his tongue."
Stanley Love *Mike Love's brother*

"They were there to lock him in his room , beat him up if they had to, and
physically restrain him."
Bob Levine *personal and business manager, on trying to stop Dennis'
drinking habits*

"I took anything to get me high. I took my dose of LSD and it shattered
my mind, but thank God I came back. Cocaine at first was a beautiful high,
but the comedown was awful. Heaven and hell. I lived in my room for
a few years and became very paranoid. But that period is over. I feel very
inspired now, and I'm even cutting down on cigarettes."
Brian Wilson, *1977*

"So between drugs, alcohol and cigarettes I totally escaped. And I found
eating to be a way of escape. You can throw that in there. That's number
four. That's how I dealt with it. I don't have drugs to escape with. Now I
have to do it on the natch. Oh, I use medicine. I'm administered medicine.
But very mild. It's for my nerves, to keep me calm. It's natural medicine.
Not like downers or uppers or any of those. It's natural medicine, safe
medicine. It's not very toxic."
Brian Wilson, *1988*

Brian's Problems

"I was very close to Brian... I was with him the day he couldn't continue any longer. I was with him in the morning and I knew that it wasn't just that he was copping out... he couldn't take it any longer."
Carl Wilson

"It was really my fault because I was hiding in my bedroom from the world. Basically I had just gotten out of commission. I mean I was out of it. I was unhealthy, overweight, I was totally a vegetable... In other words, my life got all screwed up... It happened through my starting to take drugs. I started taking a lot of cocaine and a lot of drugs and it threw me inward. I imploded. I withdrew from society through drugs and continued to do so for two, three, four years... I made everybody angry at me because I wasn't able to work, to get off my butt. Goin' to parties..."
Brian Wilson

"He was sensitive to the point of being unbalanced. He was esoteric and very eccentric. If he wanted to play ping-pong at eleven-thirty at night, he'd knock on the neighbours' door and get them out of bed to play ping-pong."
Gary Usher *friend and musician*

"I was run down mentally and emotionally because I was running around, jumping on jets from one city to another, on one night stands, also producing, writing, arranging, singing, planning, teaching – to the point where I had no peace of mind and no chance to actually sit down and think or even rest. I was so mixed up and so overworked. We were going to Houston to kick off a two week tour. I said goodbye to Marilyn, we weren't getting along too good. The plane had only been in the air five minutes when I told Al Jardine I was going to crack up any minute, but he told me to cool it. Then I started crying, I put a pillow over my face and began screaming and yelling, and I started telling people I wasn't getting off the plane. I was getting far out, coming undone, having a breakdown, and I just let myself go completely. The rubber band had stretched as far as it would go."
Brian Wilson, *1964*

Left: Brian with Dr Eugine Landy.

"The gruelling touring life; that's a strain on the nervous system.
The worst part of it was the loud sounds that came out on the stage.
See, I have only one ear that works, so I have twice as much sound
going in one ear, and all that sound drove me nuts, drove me to a
nervous breakdown.

"I just remember that I started to flip out and I slammed the door
on Carl (Wilson) and said, 'Get out of here. I don't want to see anybody'.
I told an airline stewardess that I didn't want any food, to get away from
me, things like that. I was crying on the plane and everything. That was
the start of the secluded period, which ended with *California Girls*.

"Then I had another nervous breakdown in 1972, after we went to
Holland. I'd been away from home too long. See, my wife pulled our
studio out of my house in '72, so in June of '72 we all hauled off to
Holland and built a studio, did some recording and ended up staying five
and half months. Well, as a combination of things that happened over
there, plus being away from home, I had a little breakdown over there.
I couldn't take the idea of being away from home that long.
I'm almost a Cancer, I'm June 20th, so I have a little Cancer in me,
which is very devoted to home and wanting to stay there. The security
is the home."
Brian Wilson, *1976*

"He had fits of uncontrollable anger. Then he'd fall apart and start crying during playbacks of certain tracks... what I saw appalled me."
Tony Asher *composer and co-writer of* **Pet Sounds,** *describing working on the album with Brian Wilson*

"(Brian) used to talk a lot of totter about health food (while he was) digging into a big fat hamburger. And gymnasiums! I was fitter than he was... Going on about vitamins. I thought maybe he was being amusing, you see. Having a meal with him was like the Mad Hatter's tea party: 'Have some more tea, there isn't any'."
Derek Taylor *publicist*

"When you love someone as much as I loved Brian, you begin to accept more and more. Maybe more than you should."
Marilyn Wilson

"I never considered him sick. Because what is sick to most people is they just don't know how to accept the unusual, the eccentric."
Marilyn Wilson, *1976*

"Brian, I'm sorry, he is a put-on... He's really a very highly evolved person... and he's very sensitive at the same time, which can be confusing. Brian's Brian, y'know?"
Carl Wilson

"He was not the same person I fell in love with. He had started changing little by little. He was not the same Brian that he was before the drugs..."
Marilyn Wilson, *1965*

*The controversial Dr. Eugene Landy was hired to cure Brian
for the first time by Marilyn Wilson at the end of 1975. The Beach
Boys and Marilyn Wilson fired Landy over Christmas 1976 because
they believed he was exerting too much control. Various psychiatrists
were hired in the interim but Brian returned to substance abuse
and withdrew into himself even more than before. Dr. Landy was
then hired again by Marilyn and Carl Wilson in April 1983.
Miraculously, Brian regained body and mind a second time.
Unfortunately the scenario has been played out a third time, with
Dr. Landy signing a separation agreement, held by Carl Wilson on
April 1, 1991.*

"The thing that made me go to Dr. Landy was I couldn't stand
to see Brian, who I just love and adore, unhappy with himself and
not really creating. Because music is his whole life, that's number
one to him. So one of my girlfriends told me about Dr Landy, and
I went and talked to him for an hour. I said, 'I need someone
who's gonna go to him, not where he had to go to you, because
he won't do it'. And Dr Landy said, 'Yeah, I think I can do it'.
When I met Dr Landy, I knew I'd met someone who could play
Brian's game."
Marilyn Wilson *who later was instrumental in trying to
prevent Dr Landy from treating Brian, 1976*

"He wasn't relating on the level in society where we have
expectancies of what we expect people to do. When you pick the
phone up, (you are expected) to say hello. If you do something
different, depending how different, you frighten people around you.
And if you're frightened yourself, you simply withdraw."
Dr Landy, *1976*

"Somebody should talk to him! You know what he told me?
He said, 'Okay, we're gonna start on self-nourishment'. I didn't
know what that was. He said, 'Read this little paper'. He handed
me the piece of paper and said, 'Read it to me'. It said, 'I love
you'. You're supposed to read the paper three times a day for
five minutes each time, no matter where you are, saying, 'I love you,
I love you', to yourself... Heck I lost the paper. I thought the guy
was crazy."
Brian Wilson *on Dr Landy, 1976*

"It took a while for Brian to get shipshape again, and he could
still stand to lose a few pounds of gut. But I think I understand
why he took off for a few years. He wanted to rest and felt there
was no sense living in the past. He's been through a lot of
tremendous emotional changes and setbacks from taking drugs
and not understanding them, among other things. Brian's a
reclusive, sensitive, vulnerable guy and he was probably one of
the most famous people in the world at one point. That completely
got to him."
Dennis Wilson, *1976*

"I was retreating for a while. I was convinced I was happy, but the psychiatrist convinced me otherwise. I no longer have him constantly with me. I just call him up now and then if I need him. I feel I can cope with things in my own mind now. I don't really like performing. The only thing that makes me happy now is writing."
Brian Wilson, *1977*

"I'm confused with everything that is happening around me."
Brian Wilson, *1977*

"In my programme with (Dr Landy) I was being monitored every twenty minutes by him. (He had) control of my life legally through the commitment of my wife – my wife committed me to him – 'cause I had gotten very low with drugs and got myself in a bad position, mentally, physically and emotionally. I was taken over by a doctor and I straightened up. He definitely helped me. It cost over a hundred thousand dollars – he charged me a hell of a lot per month."
Brian Wilson *on the first departure of Dr Landy*

"I much prefer the past, it was much happier."
Brian Wilson, *1977*

"I think every brilliant person pays a price for that brilliance that they're born with. I just don't think you can be a happy-go-lucky person and write music that way. Brian stopped seeing his original doctor because he brought Brian so far that Brian didn't think he needed him. 'I feel great!' Since then Brian's put on weight, he's not participating as much as we all would like him to. Brian's under a doctor's care because he gets very depressed – it's very hard being Brian Wilson. I just keep thinking of that song he wrote called *I Just Wasn't Made For These Times* – maybe he should have been born 150 years ago, and conducted an orchestra playing his symphonies. Maybe that would've been better for him. He's that brilliant."
Bruce Johnston, *1979*

"The doctor is absolutely necessary. The spectre of drugs has ruined many people, including Brian. He's still paying the dues."
Mike Love, *1980*

"Brian and I are partners in life."
Dr Landy, *1988*

"Dr Landy is a total life expert. He's an expert on life. He's an expert
on music and he's an expert on production. And he's an expert on
executive production... How? He just did. He came into his own all of
a sudden. He came out of nowhere to take over my life."
Brian Wilson, *1988*

"It worked out well. We worked together on the lyrics, but he would
fine tune them on his own. He would have a technique where he would
take the lyrics and then adjust them and send them back to my house.
I would check them out to see if I liked them. And if I liked them, we
would go with that set of lyrics. Then we made a decision to leave those
as the final lyrics. Sometimes he would even change them again from
what we had to even more fine tuning in the studio. He changed them
while I was in the studio singing, up to the minute. I mean, it was like
that close to the minute what was happening."
Brian Wilson, *1988*

"I was always allowed to do whatever I wanted to do. All of a sudden I realized I had all the freedom, and it was hard to deal with it. I had money and success and everybody was scared of me. Then all of a sudden I got zapped. The freedom got taken away like that! But I think the doctor is trying to rehabilitate me in order to bring out some of my talent that's been buried."
Brian Wilson

"Dr Landy is my daily planner, my executive producer, my lyric-writing partner and my business partner; he's the sole person who got me back."
Brian Wilson, *1988*

"I thought Brian was a perfect gentleman, apart from buttering his head and trying to put it between two slices of bread."
Tom Petty *after eating with Brian at a Los Angeles restaurant*

"I get calls in my head, from people in the vicinity or maybe ten, twenty miles out. They get to me. They say things like, 'You're going to get it, you motherfucker!' Cruel talk. That's a drag."
Brian Wilson, *1988*

"I've developed a much stronger life over the last six years since
I've come with Dr Landy. Because I had to, in order to make sense of
something that doesn't seem like it's going to be made sense of. You do
it anyway. I don't know if it's will power or just true ability with words.
I guess it's a little of each. See, when I talk about words in a literal sense.
Not like esoteric words that trigger off fantasies and strange
realities. Words that create dark sketches of meanings I don't go into.
I stick with a logical and sane approach to words and it works for me
that way."
Brian Wilson, *1988*

"Carl and my mother and Mike Love. I think they're trying to
get Gene out of there. My brother Carl never liked Gene anyway.
He and Gene never got along. If I could, I'd wring Carl's neck.
He makes me mad."
Brian Wilson, *1988*

"This is to advise you that your services as an employee of Brother
Records Inc. has been terminated, effective immediately... this action
is taken in your best interest, and is not reversible. We wish you the best
of health."
Alan Jardine, Mike Love, Carl Wilson and Dennis Wilson *in a*
letter sent to **Brian Wilson***, 1982. It was actually a hoax devised by*
The Beach Boys to get him away from his girl friend **Carolyn Williams**
whom they thought was doing him more harm than good

"I began to think that people only liked me because I was famous.
I felt like I couldn't trust anybody in the whole world. I couldn't trust
people with my feelings. Every time I turned around, I'd get my feelings
hurt. The fact that I didn't trust people drove me nuts. I kind of broke
down. I cracked up."
Brian Wilson, *1988*

"He's my boss, and I like him as my boss. I'm in step with Gene.
He gets what he wants. I just toe the line."
Brian Wilson *on Dr Landy's control, 1988*

"Gene told me that the programme was legally over about two
months ago. But I don't believe that I could walk away. First of all,
I'd be afraid. I'd be scared. I wouldn't know where to live; I wouldn't
know how to live."
Brian Wilson, *1988*

"I feel like a prisoner, and I don't know when it's going to end.
He'd put the police on me if I took off... and he'd put me on a funny
farm... He's always got that threat of putting me on the funny farm."
Brian Wilson, *1988*

"I was in such a hole that I swear to God every living second of my
life was just a disastrous calamity."
Brian Wilson

"No one thought there was hope for Brian, but four people decided to take the shot anyhow: his brother Carl; Carl's manager, Jerry Schilling; Brian's lawyer, John Branca; and The Beach Boys' manager, Tom Hulett. They got together in January 1983, took Brian away from these other people, and called me. I said, 'There are certain conditions. I want him in hospital first; I want to check the man out physically.

"We put Brian through every test imaginable to see what food allergies he had, the levels of medication in his blood stream. This man was on so much shit! He had forty percent lung capacity and no liver!"
Dr Landy, *1985*

"We all have a success mechanism. Dr Landy has put that in me."
Brian Wilson, *1987*

"I want to be able to pop out of bed at six or seven in the morning and meet the day. But I can't. I'm negatively programmed to think that each day is a bummer."
Brian Wilson, *1988*

"I think he takes a lot of shit from writers and from my family and that he's being treated unfairly. They're not getting the full picture of what really happened with Dr Landy and me – just part of the picture. They're uninformed as to what has really occurred. I feel bad about it. I feel bad for Gene because he has to sit there and take that shit. He doesn't deserve it. He deserves more credit than he's getting."
Brian Wilson, *1988*

"I'm scared of Gene. Obviously. What's there to be scared of? Nothing really. Kind of a nightmare that's gonna get easier. I hope."
Brian Wilson, *1988*

"I have a series of reality checks. Am I still in reality, or am I going off into fantasy? "
Brian Wilson, *1988*

"God, I'm so thankful that I have a doctor, you know? Then I go through periods where I think, 'Goddamn, he's doing nothing but restricting my mind!' It's paradoxical, I know, and I feel an inner battle. Today I want to go places. I want to go to Danny Hutton's house , but I can't because of the doctor. I feel like a prisoner, and I don't know when it's going to end. With doctors on your ass, it's impossible to make a move. I can write when I want, but I can't go into the studio unless they tell me I can."
Brian Wilson

"He's classified as a paranoid schizophrenic. Paranoia meaning fear, and schizophrenia meaning you look at things a little differently than the normal person does. And therefore Brian is just unable to cope with a lot of things in life; as a result he became a recluse and did all those weird things that the press seem to love to print about 20 years later."
Mike Love, *1993*

Charles Manson

"Fear is nothing but awareness. I was only frightened as a child because I did not understand fear – the dark, being lost, what was under the bed! It came from within. Sometimes the wizard frightens me – Charlie Manson who is another friend of mine who says he is God and the Devil! He sings, plays and writes poetry and may be another artist for Brother Records."
Dennis Wilson

"I was absolutely horrified, terrified. First of all, when Manson and his family, the girls, moved in with Dennis, Dennis had this beautiful place at Will Rogers State Park, right off Sunset, and he befriended them. They were just hippies and he thought Manson was the nicest person, a very gentle, nice guy. Murry had a fit, because he knew there were a bunch of girls living there. I went there one day. Dennis was at the recording studio in Brian's house, and he asked me if I'd take him home. I was very hesitant because I thought Murry wouldn't like it, but I took him home, and he said, 'Will you just come in and meet them? Come on, they're nice'. So I went in, and Charlie Manson was walking through this big yard with a long robe on, and Dennis introduced me.
  "I just thought he looked older than he supposedly is, like an older man, and I thought he had a kind face. That was the only impression I had. And I did think they were a bunch of leeches; Dennis had been through that before. He could never stand to see anyone who needed anything or anybody who had any kind of problem – he was right there. Then when that horrible story came out about Manson's arrest for the Sharon Tate murder, Annie (Carl's wife) called me. I didn't connect at all that was the same person and the same family who had been with Dennis. When she told me I just totally froze. When they left Dennis's house, Manson or somebody stole Dennis's Ferrari, and they stole everything in the house that could be moved. Everything. Stripped. Dennis had kicked them out because they were into heavy drugs, and he just wanted them out."
Audree Wilson

Right: Dennis with Karen Lamm.

"Charlie struck me as a very intense and dogmatic type. I didn't want nothing to do with Charlie. He was living with Dennis at the time. Dennis was just divorced; I suppose the life-style appealed to him. Perhaps I have more sexual inhibitions, moral structures. I wasn't into drugs at that point, which was Charlie's way of conditioning his little friends, turning them into egoless entities. I wasn't going for his pitch.

"Dennis ran up the largest gonorrhoea bill in history the time the whole family got the clap. He took them all to a Beverly Hills doctor – it took something like a thousand dollars in penicillin.

"We've got several eight-track tapes of Charlie and the girls that Dennis cut, maybe even some sixteen-track. Just chanting, fucking, sucking, barfing. Maybe we'll put it out in the Fall. Call it *Death Row*.

"Just say Dennis was the farthest out in life-style of any of us, having known Charles Manson before he made the headlines. And that he requested you do not bring it up."
Anonymous Beach Boy

"No. Never. As long as I live I'll never talk about that. I don't know anything, you know? If I did, I would've been up on that witness stand."
Dennis Wilson

Death Of Dennis

When Dennis was in financial trouble he was forced to sell his boat Harmony. *He died while visiting a friend who lived on a boat docked in the same quay as* Harmony.

After drinking liquor to stay warm in the water Dennis repeatedly dived to reclaim objects he recalled throwing off the side of his old boat. One of his dives ended up being his last.

Dennis drowned in 12 feet of water on December 28, 1983. He was 39. He had always said he wanted to be buried at sea, and according to his wish he was returned to the ocean three days later. President Ronald Reagan arranged for Dennis to be buried at sea because Federal law prohibits sea burials.

"They say I live a fast life. Maybe I just like a fast life. I wouldn't give it up for anything in the world. It won't last for ever, either. But the memories will."
Dennis Wilson

"Carlos told me there was a message on my answer phone at this other house down the street that we used to live at. I went in there and this guy Jerry Schilling, who's Carl's manager, told me, 'I'm sorry to have to tell you that Dennis drowned'."
Brian Wilson, *1985*

"I felt real strange. It's a weird feeling when you hear about a death in the family, a weird trip. It's not something you can really talk about or describe. I got tears after about a half-hour. Then I saw it on the news and thought, 'Oh God, there he is, lying there dead'. I was blown out by the whole idea that he drowned, although I just let it lay, I didn't fuck with it. I didn't think too much about it. I let it lay... It pissed me off when he drowned because I wasn't just losing a brother I was losing a friend, and that compounded it even more. "
Brian Wilson, *1984*

"I told Brian I thought the best thing we could do was write a song for Dennis. (However) we didn't work on it that night. We just talked and toasted in the New Year. We were all so much a part of each other that I'm sure we'll miss him every single day the rest of our lives. There's no way we'll not miss him."
Mike Love, *1983*

"The idea of disbanding never came up really. We just want to take some time for our hearts to mend and start 1984 on a very positive note."
Carl Wilson, *1983*

"We're quite well-equipped to perform. But emotionally, right now, we wanted to wait a little before we sing *Fun Fun Fun* again."
Mike Love, *1983*

"We all lived this wonderful life with The Beach Boys. And up until December 28, we lived it with Dennis Wilson."
Mike Love

"Really positive, and wholesome, and fun. And all our adult lives we performed to totally project a good time. And that's what we're going to do in the future."
Mike Love, *1983*

"I disagree with the burial at sea. I thought that took on a very scary effect. Burying out at sea just didn't seem like the proper way to bury somebody. I went through a lot of changes there."
Brian Wilson, *1983*

Finances

"An interviewer once asked me if money is my incentive to write music. The answer is no. I've never written one note or word of music simply because I think it will make money."
Brian Wilson, *1965*

"I don't think you'll get anywhere in this business if you only think about the money. But you won't get anywhere if you don't think about it at all..."
Bruce Johnston, *1967*

"If we don't pick ourselves off our backsides and have a hit record soon we will be in (even) worse trouble. We all know that if we don't watch it and do something drastic, in a few months we won't have a penny in the bank."
Brian Wilson, *1969*

"If I want money I come into the office and get it. I gave away
everything, even my gold records. I don't have a car. If I need a ride
I hitch a lift. All I need is a big surfboard and a piano. I just don't dig
marriage – although Carl does."
Dennis Wilson, *1969*

"I know that there was a thing where Brian kept on giving people
money to 'score'. Not for himself, but for themselves. It's like he was
giving a guy every week a few hundred bucks, and a very well-known guy
at that. I won't mention his name, because I don't want to damage him.
   "And so what the business office did was they put Brian's wife...
ah, took Brian's signature off the cheques for a while until he could
be a little more responsible about it."
Carl Wilson, *1976*

"I didn't know how to handle money. Getting money – that was really
hard for me to accept."
Brian Wilson, *1976*

"Let me say this. I don't agree with the Wilsons' personal philosophy.
I'm an opportunist and I'm greedy on a sensible level. I take every kind
of advantage, which they don't. So does Mike Love. Mike's a lot cooler.
But the others don't like to hustle. Time means nothing to them.
I think, here's something that'll bring another fifteen or twenty
thousand dollars, but as often as not they'd rather sit home than do
a concert. Some of them have houses up on Beverly Hills. If they were
normal Americans they'd only have two weeks off a year. The rest of
the time they'd be making money."
Bruce Johnston

"I don't really care for the business side of things that much, I'm just not that type. I'm not a good business man. I like being a recording artiste but I don't like dealing with numbers or money like a banker. When you get down to it, with being a good businessman it's not so much what you can earn, but how much you can do and how it all ends up."
Carl Wilson

"I worry about money, although I don't make much any more, not like I used to. I make enough money to pay my bills and keep a few cents in the bank. I'm a millionaire on paper."
Brian Wilson, *1988*

"I formulated the band. I made them famous, and they know it and are appreciative of it. They pay me one fourth of all the income of the tours that they take."
Brian Wilson, *1988*

The Slump

"The Beach Boys went through a big slump. This is what happened.
At the end of the 60s there was a transition from surfin', and the record
companies were so used to promoting us as surfers that they didn't
realise things were changing.

   "With people like Jimi Hendrix coming up, it was an image
that was extremely difficult for us to try and outlive. It was a time
of great change and we found it almost impossible to shake off our
old identity."
Dennis Wilson, *1977*

"I guess, maybe the people who normally buy records just didn't
want to buy ours... it's hard to try and understand why... truthfully,
I dunno."
Dennis Wilson, *1977*

"We (The Beach Boys) got worn out. We had been under pressure
all those years to prove our greatness and to keep our place and our
stature in the business. By 1972, we'd gotten to a point where we were
a little bit fatigued. You could liken it to a pitcher of water. You slowly
pour the water out and finally there's no more water until you fill it
back up."
Brian Wilson

"I'd put it much stronger than that, they (the public) ignored us.
There's no use denying it, we went suddenly from being a very large
group into being a small group again. It broke my heart . It hurt.
It's no use me saying it didn't. Believe me, it really does hurt to
suddenly realise that you're not what you used to be. And that people
don't want to know."
Dennis Wilson, *1977*

"We made records, singles for the kids, but they didn't buy them.
For a couple of years in a row, '69 and '70, the singles just didn't
make it. We thought that they were great, we figured that they were
super... I think the kids left us... I felt blue. I felt upset that they
didn't make it... I just thought that they could have, should have...
They were beautiful but they didn't go as well as we thought."
Brian Wilson

"The Beach Boys just sort of foundered for a while there. They weren't
really happening; they really weren't that big of a group for a while,
you know?"
Brian Wilson, *1988*

"I lost interest in writing songs. I lost the inspiration. I was too
concerned with getting drugs to write songs."
Brian Wilson, *1988*

ON EACH OTHER

"He's very vulnerable. He would lay down his life for a butterfly...
He's had a very tragic life emotionally. I remember in sixth grade...
Brian used to sing in school. He sang very high and his buddies that
he'd hang out with laughed at him. He ran home from school, and
I chased after him. It broke my heart to see him emotionally involved
in the music at such an early age and to have his friends laugh at him,
call him a girl or something. But every time he's ever stuck it out, put it
out for people to see, to share it with people, a lot of time he has
been hurt. Or maybe people just didn't understand him."
Dennis Wilson *on Brian*

"Brian is a dedicated genius. He composes all our material. He's had
collaboration assists with some lyrics but he writes all the music and
arrangements. I don't know how he finds time to do it all. He just calls
us and says, 'I just wrote another song. Let's record it'."
Carl Wilson, *1965*

"Al was away for about a year. He had pretensions, ideas of going to a
dental school. But soon he figured that he could look down a whole lot
more mouths at one time on stage with The Beach Boys than at one time
in a dentist's chair."
Mike Love *on Al Jardine*

"I think there are probably times when all of us... well we can't have...
well we've had our share you know... all the things but... er well we've
known each other for a really long time so when you grow up together
you accept each other... you know as you are and so you know having
that understanding of each other... we just... and it really is great.
A great deal of fellowship in the group... in a very cool way. It's just there
as if it should happen. We've been through an awful lot you know...
together as people, so that type of thing, you know, makes a bond with
people... So that's part of the reason. But the main reason is music."
Carl Wilson

"The boys are the greatest. I couldn't be happier with any other combination of players-singers. Above all, we take enormous pride in our
concerts and records. We intend to stay on top of the pop chart heap."
Brian Wilson, *1965*

"No, not with one ear. Only one works, you know. He had an operation
but it wasn't successful at the time. Whenever his ear is fatigued, his bad
ear, his right ear, will start to work. But it will be very painful and sound
very low fidelity, like one of those tin can walkie-talkies, you know?
That's how he explained it anyway, and he gets out of balance and
everything. It's been that way for many years. Ever since he was
an infant."
Carl Wilson *on Brian*

"It takes a long time for Brian to accept you. He distrusts you, then likes you, he's suspicious of you, until you finally become accepted by him."
Bruce Johnston, *1967*

"The others never telephone me. But then I suppose we have very little in common. They're all married and have their own circle of friends and I have mine. They ask me around for dinner occasionally but I seldom manage to make it."
Bruce Johnston, *1967*

"Oh, he exists all right, look around you he's everywhere."
Dennis Wilson *asked if Brian was alive and well, 1970*

"I love him very much. One of the most talented people I know. He's just out of the race, ahead of all."
Carl Wilson *on Brian, 1971*

"People always thought Brian was a good time guy until he started releasing those heavy, searching songs on *Pet Sounds* 'n' all, but that stuff was closer to his own personality and perceptions. By the time people get close to an accurate picture of Brian Wilson – if ever – he's gonna be far beyond them again, and I can dig his frustration."
Dennis Wilson, *1976*

"We've missed him a lot. After all his music has been 99% responsible for our success. I think any creative person has low times when they stay in the background for a while. That's what Brian's been doing. All that stuff about the sand boxes is true. We have even had business meetings in a tent in his den. But what people don't realise is the sense of humour behind it."
Carl Wilson *on Brian*

"Everything I do is a stepping stone from Brian – he's taught me so much."
Dennis Wilson, *1977*

"We had our chart done once... it mentioned in there that Brian and I were brothers in a past life and that Mike and I were also related in the past. But Brian and I came from such different backgrounds in this life; I came from the mid-west and Brian grew up in Hawthorne, California. Our only similarities are in music."
Al Jardine, *1977*

"He is a master, musically. I am dumbfounded at him. I am in awe of him. I've grown up with him and watched him go through changes, and he is the most vulnerable human being I know. The depth of that guy... I mean... he changed the world with his influence. I'm devoting my life to Brian on a musical level, and the rest of the group feel the same way. When Brian plays something for us, we just gape. It gets very emotional."
Dennis Wilson *on Brian*

"Brian Wilson is not a good looking human being, yet his music is beautiful. Look at Nat King Cole – he looked like a real piece of shit but he had a beautiful voice. Look at Aretha Franklin – she would scare me in a dark room, yet her voice is fantastic. Roy Orbison too. The thing I to listen to is the music."
Dennis Wilson, *1976*

"I read an album proposal that Brian wanted to do on 'Helpful Hints.' I read the first two lines of the thing and fell on the floor laughing... He was serious, he wanted to do it as an album project. How you put it into an album I'll never know. There were hints about how to dress faster. You find a top and practise shooting your arm in and out of the sleeve. He said that if you could practise this, it will save you many valuable seconds when you're late for work. Also, there was a part on how to lunge for falling objects. You crouch down like this and then spring for it. He had some drink in the proposal too. How to stir it up and don't cheat and stuff. The whole thing was typed out one night, that's the kind of guy he is – completely maniacal, humorous, just deadpan."
Mike Love

"The thing I wonder about is where does Brian's creative spark come from? Not his subjects or anything, but his spark. What makes it so great for me is that I really don't know. There's a mystery behind Brian, even to me. Creatively, where in the fuck does the guy go? Where is he coming from?"
Dennis Wilson, *1976*

"Dennis is not a kind of person who you can give another chance. He's not the kind of person who's trustworthy. People who like drugs lie, they are not trustworthy. I can dig it because... I'm an addictive personality but I am addicted to TM and meditate my ass off."
Mike Love *on Dennis*

"Around the time when we put out the first live Beach Boys album (1964) , we were doing a show with striped shirts on and the whole bit, and I found myself totally gazing at Brian, thinking, 'This guy's my brother? I was famous because some guy was 'beautiful', and I got the chance to play drums and sing with him and take part in this great ride – God, what a fuckin' honour!"
Dennis Wilson, *1977*

"They are my family. It is very difficult just to make a statement about what they mean to me. I love them all. As a person I'm outwardly more quiet than the others, probably a little calmer. I've never written music or poetry or painted – all my creative outlets are involved in being a member of the group. Brian and I are very close. He always plays me everything he writes and we talk about it."
Carl Wilson

"As an artist, and I'm speaking for myself, I have always been a little intimidated by Brian's talent. It's like if you're in a team and the person who plays in the position you prefer also happens to be a far superior player. You tend to stand back and help his game. And like I've already stated, Brian is The Beach Boys."
Dennis Wilson, *1977*

"Brian is an anachronism in his own time. You accept him for what he is. If he says he is coming to the studio, you stop what you are doing and go, because when he does something, he does it for keeps. But today he's a short-distance runner. He's not running the 440 at this stage of his life. But he's a killer in the 100 yard dash."
Al Jardine, *1978*

"He doesn't tolerate any bullshit from any of us – he keeps us in shape and he's very well organised... he's got briefcases full of lyrics and ideas."
Carl Wilson *on Mike Love, 1980*

"He's a great singer, a great emcee and a great looking guy. Unfortunately, he does have a little problem with his hair, but that's just to keep him going. You know why God did that to him, don't you? So he won't quit. So he'll be tough and say, 'Goddamn! I'm going to get this right if it kills me'."
Brian Wilson *on Mike Love, 1988*

"He doesn't want to get locked into a particular mode. He gets bored very easily... and that probably is why his music has retained through the years a feeling of freshness and spontaneity... because you never find Brian doing an eight-minute riff on anything."
Mike Love

"Speaking for myself, musically I'm most influenced by Brian. I mean that's obvious. And I've been writing a lot of songs lately. Dennis is writing a lot of beautiful music, and Brian's writing some beautiful songs. Everybody's writing. I don't know exactly what's gonna happen yet I just know there's gonna be a lot of music."
Carl Wilson

"For me The Beach Boys are among my very hardest people in the world to be with. I find it more difficult to be with The Beach Boys over, say, 95% of the people I know in the whole world."
Brian Wilson, *1988*

"We'd be in the studio and he would play us a song, we'd start crying it was so great... I mean it was like 'how could this possibly be happening. How'd you write that?' There is not one person in the group that could come close to Brian's talent!"
Dennis Wilson *on Brian*

"You know what I think? What's going to happen to The Beach Boys is that one day Brian Wilson will be the only one left. I'm sure he's going to be like Stravinsky eventually. He's been recognized already for his genius. He won't stay doing what he is. He'll go on to other things."
Bruce Johnston

"I love The Beach Boys and I like being with them, although sometimes I feel that I'm uncomfortable with them. Let's drop that subject, 'cause that's a rough one. That's the one subject that I wish I could master. If I could just master that and get it all together. Someday I will."
Brian Wilson, 1988

"He and I were buddies when we first started out. We'd go fishing together, went surfing a couple of times, we'd go on trips here and there along the California coastline. We'd race our cars – he had a Stingray and I had an XKE – so we had a lot of fun together in the early days of the group. Then around the *Pet Sounds* era, he started getting involved in the same type of medicaments that my cousin Brian did, but Dennis's nature is different to Brian's, he's more of a rebel, more physically aggressive and stuff. Nobody could tell him what to do. If you told him, 'Hey Dennis, maybe it wouldn't be good to drink two bottles of whatever it was, or take all those drugs he would not listen to you on purpose."
Mike Love *on the endless feud between him and Dennis.*
Mike was furious when Dennis married Mike's illegitimate daughter Shawn, 1993

UP TO THE PRESENT

"We're coming into our twenty-fifth anniversary. It's been a long time since Brian chased me halfway across the campus at El Camino college and asked me to start a garage band with his brothers. When I wrote *California Calling*, a neo-classical surfing song, with Brian, so many great memories flooded back: me teaching *Sloop John B* to the band, Brian hiring the theremin player (Paul Tanner) for *Good Vibrations*, Mike cutting *I Get Around*. I'm still glad I left dental school, still thrilled to be a Beach Boy."
Al Jardine, *1985*

"I want to shave my beard soon, practise hard and get back into action with people like David Bowie and Cyndi Lauper. I'm not worried. Years ago, The Beatles sensation made me a little bit jealous and uncertain for The Beach Boys' well-being and our future, but after about a year of surviving The Beatles I realised that we could stand on our own. I feel that way now. I want to get my solo album out by the end of the year. First The Beach Boys album, and then come back with mine. And I'd like to meet Madonna! I'd say, 'Gee, you're pretty!' I seriously doubt she's a virgin, but that's a good song."
Brian Wilson, *1985*

"Brian took us to a new high aurally with *Pet Sounds*, and then we had a breakthrough again with *Sunflower*. *The Beach Boys* is a new chapter, a marriage of 'The Beach Boys' vocabulary with playing and arranging of the 1980's. The first songs on each side, *Getcha Back* and *California Calling* are what you expect from the band, yet so fresh."
Bruce Johnston, *1985*

"As for The Beach Boys, we're very much a vital band again, and we're also taking advantage of the most advanced recording technology once more – that was always a facet of the best stuff we've done in the past. The digital approach is so new and it can be quite tedious until you learn it."
Carl Wilson, *1985*

"I offered to produce their next album and they turned me down. So we might go our separate ways. I'd prefer to continue with The Beach Boys, because that's a bigger name, but if we split up I won't cry."
Brian Wilson, *1987*

"It's the same old thing. We don't get a chance to see him, so I don't know. He's totally under Landy's control."
Carl Wilson, *1987*

"My private life has become my career. I'm too on top of it musically
to ever quit."
Brian Wilson, *1987*

"We're all used to getting our own way pretty much. And we're all
somewhat forceful, although I've never been a person using a lot of
force pushing to get my way. You could get the idea that there is a lot
of dissension in the group, that we're going 98 different directions.
It's an unusual story."
Carl Wilson, *1987*

"It gets a little hot and sticky in a group, you know, in a famous group.
Egos get a little weird and little signals like 'Stay away!' You know?
We're saying 'Stay away' to each other. We're at a weird place in our
career now. It's not a real comfortable phase, you know what I mean?"
Brian Wilson, *1988*

"There are so many mixed feelings in The Beach Boys that I can't
handle it; I don't like it. I don't like the way it feels, so I canned it
and said I don't want to do very many shows with them.
    "I stopped worrying about Mike Love and Carl Wilson and those guys,
and started worrying about myself. When I show up to a concert,
I feel their resentment. I feel like they think, 'Oh, he gets to come out
whenever he wants to, but we have to work all year. I think The Beach
Boys are playing fear games with me."
Brian Wilson, *1988*

"I was going down a long poison road. Drugs, bad foods, no exercise,
smoking, drinking. I was an alcoholic for many years. I don't do any
of those things any more. I feel great. I haven't felt this good since
I was 24 – the year I made *Good Vibrations*."
Brian Wilson, *1988*

"We made a plastic, contrived record here and there. I think we're
respected as a group that made good records, but there are records that
I'm sorry I put my name on."
Brian Wilson, *1988*

"I was thinking, hey man, what's wrong with me? I can't seem to write
a song here. I'd plunk something out on the piano – 'God-dammit, no!'
I'd shut the piano down. I'd take my hands and just pound on the keys
for a couple of minutes to try to get all that frustration out of me.
It was there. It was just lying dormant. It was unharnessed creativity.
I still had it inside of me. You never lose that."
Brian Wilson, *1988*

"I'd rather do a solo album career. I like The Beach Boys and I like
recording with them. But as people we don't get along, you know?
We don't call each other enough to constitute real relationships,
you know? And that's all because of the success we've shared."
Brian Wilson, *1988*

"The Beach Boys probably feel a little shackled too when every night they've got to do *409* and *Shut Down* and *Surfin' Safari*. They have to do all those songs and they hate it, but that's what made 'em famous so they've got to do it. I think the guys would much rather do some of the album cuts that we've done over the years, but they do those old songs that sound for shit. They sound real stupid."
Brian Wilson, *1988*

"Well, yeah, I've had obstacles in my life. And I have a name to live up to. That alone was a hardship for me, living up to my name. Goddamn was it hard."
Brian Wilson, *1988*

"Music is always with me. I always have some song I'm humming or whistlin', you know? Music is just like beauty or happiness. It's beauty."
Brian Wilson

"Our personal relationships aren't working. Do you know they had, or tried to have, a meeting without me? It's been four months since I've seen the other guys."
Brian Wilson, *1988*

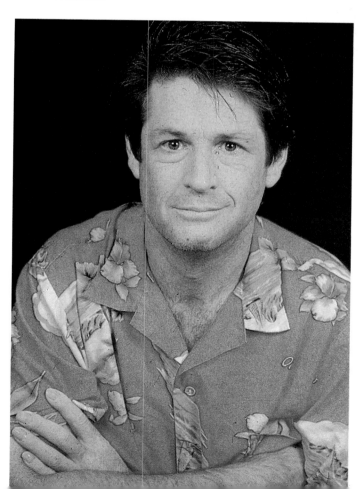

"I think about a lot of music a lot of the time. I think about music…
and I think about girls… and I think about business."
Brian Wilson, *1988*

"Brian in response to some questions about the book said 'The book
is bullshit'. He'll say one thing at one time, and another thing at
another time, so you don't really know what the truth is. But it is
interesting that he should say that. See I have a lawsuit against him for
defamation, as well as the fact that he didn't credit me for *California
Girls* and about 78 other songs that I counted, where he didn't give me
either credit or payment – like *I Get Around, Little Saint Nick, Catch
A Wave, Hawaii,* all these songs I co-authored with him, but he and
his father, my uncle Murry, dis-included me, then said for years,
'Oh, it's an oversight… We'll take care of it'. Then he studiously
avoids saying in the book that I wrote anything. There's just a snide
reference or two."
Mike Love *on Brian's autobiography* **Wouldn't It Be Nice,** *1993*

"He's a paranoid schizophrenic, and he feels guilty because he cheated
me out of millions of dollars and credit for things. His ego was distorted
at that time that he couldn't come to grips with the fact that there was
a catalyst necessary to bring out the greatness in him. It was me with the
concepts and Brian with the music, and that's where the strength lay.
I am always into the concept and the lyrics and rhymes and things that
encompass a lot of meaning… mean one thing to someone who is eight
years old and something completely different to someone 28 years old.
I am always thinking of those kinds of things when I am writing a lyric –
same as I did with *Kokomo*, which was No.1 in 1988, whereas Brian's
solo album came out and didn't have one hit record on it.
   "It's not that he couldn't be successful with somebody else, but he
hasn't had the right collaborators. You've got Gene Landy, who wants to
be a songwriter and producer and all that, but with respect to Brian's
type of creativity and psyche, as clever as Gene is about the mental
health part of it , I don't think his talents are in that direction, from
the standpoint of commercial creativity and pop music."
Mike Love, *1993*

"We're in depositions at the moment. It's like you're in trial, but you're not in front of the judge; you're going through the discovery process of what is true and what's not, to distill where things should go procedurally, legally, from there – and as part of this deposition process, I was alluding to the fact that Brian twice said, in response to the book, that the book is bullshit. So if the book is such bullshit, why did he go out and promote it and do interviews and TV talk shows? If it's bullshit, was he perpetrating a hoax upon his fans and the press and public? I guess so, because he said it was bullshit..."
Mike Love, *1993*

"I think it's difficult to promote and be commercially successful with an album that's called *Sweet Insanity*. If you look at the history of pop music, the 'troubled genius' approach hasn't really worked all that well in terms of Top 10 records. Who wants to buy an album and hear a load of songs about therapy and mental illness? I don't think that's very mainstream pop."
Mike Love *on Brian's second solo album* Sweet Insanity *which was turned down by Sire Records who deemed it not sufficiently commercial, 1993*

"I just want him to pay me, and recognise my contributions. That will absolve him of the guilt, and let him re-approach working with me and the rest of the guys. We would I'm sure, be successful, given the opportunity to work together."
Mike Love *on Brian, 1993*

AND IN MY OPINION...

"Now we'll never have to listen to surf music again."
Jimi Hendrix *after setting his guitar on fire at the* Monterey Pop Festival

"Brian is a very sweet guy and a nice human being. I'm glad he's coming out of his shell. I think he got in a trap with *Good Vibrations*. I think he got condemned more than condoned.

"He became a prisoner instead of a poet. He had the plaudits, the accolades and touched the masses. I know that music is a very important thing to him, besides a vocation. It became cluttered the last few years. Your attitude is in the grooves, and it's a very personal thing... but Brian thrived on competition.

"I remember when *Fun Fun Fun* came out. He wasn't interested in the money, but a Top Ten record. He wanted to know how the song would do against The Beatles and if KFWB (an LA radio station) would play it. But I never saw Brian as a competitor."
Phil Spector, *1977*

"He (Brian) was the first guy to do it until it was right. He damned everybody till it was right, then he gave them the record. He took his chances. A lot of us would get chicken after four hours and say, 'We better get off that tune'. Brian would hang in there for nine hours no matter what the cost. I used to think he was crazy, but he was right."
Nick Venet *who signed and produced The Beach Boys*

"*California Girls*, that's when I became romantically involved with the recording industry, and it was that as well as necessity which pushed me into it. I started out as a studio musician on that one day..."
Van Dyke Parks *co-writer of* Heroes and Villains *and the lost* Smile

Above: Jimi Hendrix.

Below: Phil Spector.

"A genius musician, but an amateur human being."
Tony Asher *producer, on Brian Wilson*

"The Beatles themselves learned a great deal from Brian Wilson's webbed hand, you know? Which at that time was looked at as clumsy or non-pianistic, but it was metronomic. The guy's an anchor, he's a spine. Anything Brian gets into has a foundation. And many people learned a lot from the way he plays piano – a lot came from that, as much as came from Tin Pan Alley. It wasn't so much a matter of notes as what was suggested by the very sound of the piano. And I met Brian just at a point during the recording of *Pet Sounds*, when the inclusion of a 'cello – which I recall was my idea – was important to the development of a record; and Brian did everything he could generously to help me along. So I became an exercising lyricist. I started writing words for him."
Van Dyke Parks *co-writer of* Heroes And Villains *and* Smile

"Music is Brian Wilson's best friend, lover, everything. On a one-to-one basis, it's the only thing that has never wronged him. It's when people, and gossip, and record companies came into play that things went askew. The music never betrayed him; it's the only thing he can trust. And given Brian's vulnerable, exclusive nature, it's only natural that it's the central fact and concern in his life. He may forget a name or a contract, but he never forgets the music. It's a consequence of devotional thinking, and geniuses are prone to it."
Van Dyke Parks *co-writer of* **Pet Sounds**

"The boys were like children... and they would do crazy things. (I'd say to them), 'You can't be Beach Boys all your life'."
Catherine Pace *Beach Boys bookkeeper*

"*Pet Sounds* was my inspiration for making *Sgt. Pepper's*... the big influence... the musical invention... was the big thing for me. I just thought, 'Dear me, this is the album of all time. What are we going to do?"
Paul McCartney

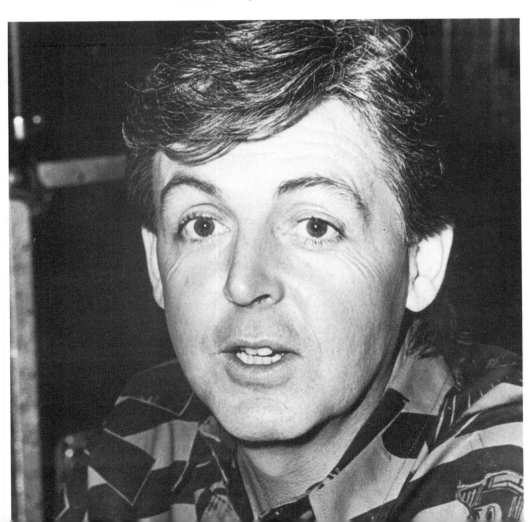